Songs and Ballads
of Dundee

Nigel Gatherer

Foreword by
Peter Shepheard

JOHN DONALD
EDINBURGH

This edition published in 2000 by John Donald
an imprint of Birlinn Limited
8 Canongate Venture
5 New Street
Edinburgh
EH8 8BH

First published in 1985 by
John Donald Publishers Limited

ISBN 0 85976 538 5

British Library Cataloguing-in-Publication Data
A catalogue record for this book is available from the British Library

Printed and bound by Redwood Books, Trowbridge

Foreword

It was in the spring of this year that I first heard about Nigel Gatherer's nearly completed work on a book of Dundee songs. I was greatly interested as I had, back in the 1960s, helped compile material for a book on just the same subject, together with Maurice Fleming, the Blairgowrie-born writer and folksong collector. But our book never reached publication.

I lived, at the time, near St. Andrews and, through the local folk club, I was able to hear and meet some of Scotland's great traditional singers when they were guests at the club – Jimmy McBeath, the north-east bothy ballad singer, Jeannie Robertson, the Aberdeen ballad singer, Willie Scott, the border shepherd, and the Stewart family of Blairgowrie.

A number of chance encounters led me to discover that Fife too had a living tradition of folksong, and between 1966 and 1968, with tape recorder over my shoulder, I recorded hundreds of songs from the travelling folk, fishermen and farm workers of Fife. I collected too from travellers in the berryfields of Blairgowrie – with the help of Belle Stewart who introduced me to her traveller friends and relatives.

In 1966, together with Maurice Fleming, I helped start the Blairgowrie Festival to provide a public platform for some of the great singers we knew existed. From this event grew the Traditional Music and Song Association of Scotland (the T.M.S.A.) which is now involved in traditional music festivals throughout the country.

The idea for a book of Dundee songs arose around this time. Maurice had recorded the song repertoire of Mary Brooksbank, author of the famous 'Jute Mill Song', and between us we had collected quite a number of songs about Dundee in Fife, Angus and Perthshire and from singers in Dundee itself. By 1969 we had put together about forty songs for the projected book, and further collecting was done in the early '70s.

That might have been the end of the story, but on hearing about Nigel Gatherer's project we offered our full co-operation. While Maurice Fleming and I had confined our work to song versions from oral tradition, Nigel's emphasis had been on printed song texts from old books, broadsides and songsheets, and he had compiled historical background to the material. So our two collections were to a large degree complementary. Where there was overlap we decided to give precedence to versions collected from tradition.

During the last month I have had a busy and exciting time contacting singers, including many of the singers we first collected from in the '60s and '70s. Several new songs or song versions have come to light – 'Sandy's Mill' from Archie Webster, and 'The Iron Horse' from Charlie Lamb as sung by his grandfather. I knew that Archie Webster and Eck

Harley both had really interesting versions of the rare but widely known ballad often called 'The blind man he can see'. These I recorded and we have given them the title 'The Wife o' Dundee'. Only a few weeks ago I was told about the 92-year-old Dundee singer Stuartie Foy, and he recorded for us his song 'Comin' Ower the Tay Brig tae Bonnie Dundee'. Also, Stewart Brown of the Lowland Folk and Jim Reid, founder of the Foundry Bar Band, have contributed several valuable songs.

I am sure there are still many songs we have missed – and we will always be keen to hear of songs and singers. But I am sure too that this book will provide some great entertainment, some good reading and I hope ensure that Dundee's songs will still be sung for many years to come.

Peter Shepheard,
Kingskettle,
Fife.
May 1985.

Acknowledgements

I am extremely grateful to the following: Catherine Smith for being such an interested and enthusiastic correspondent and informant; Agnes McIntyre and Joe McGinley for invaluable help with music problems; Dr. W. Gatherer for encouragement and Mrs J. M. Gatherer for typing; Mr Douglas Spence of the D.C. Thomson Photograph Dept., Maurice Fleming for his help and co-operation and for letting me use some of his collection of Dundee songs. I would also like to thank Maureen Rooney, Debbie Hunter and Marten Claridge. Above all, however, I am deeply indebted to Peter Shepheard for making available to me the Dundee songs in his large collection of recorded Scottish traditional music, for arranging the songs from that collection, and for generally going out of his way to help me compile this book.

I would like to thank the following singers, composers and publishers who have given permission for songs to be printed in this book:

Mrs Balfour, Lindores, Fife (14)
Stewart Brown, Dundee (25, 30a, 53)
Alec Clark, Dundee (45a)
Maurice Fleming, Blairgowrie (17, 18, 19, 21, 24, 26, 32, 37, 38, 41, 42, 43, 44, 45, 65, 66, 70, 75)
Stuartie Foy, Dundee (34c, 79)
Eck Harley, Cupar, Fife (33a, 34a, 35a, 57a, 68a)
Charlie Lamb, Lochee, Dundee (55, 63b, 67b, 73, 74, 76)
Dave Marshall (69)
Jim Reid, Dundee (5, 6, 27, 31b, 35b, 39, 54, 56, 57b, 58, 77)
Maureen Rooney, Charleston, Dundee (40)
Catherine Smith, Lochee, Dundee (78, 80)
Springthyme Music (56, 77)
Belle Stewart (31a, 63a)
Annie Watkins, Dundee (32, 41, 45b, 65, 70)
Archie Webster, Strathkinness, Fife (67, 68b, 72)
John White, Fife (33b)
David Winter & Son Ltd., Dundee (19, 21, 37, 38, 42, 43, 44, 66)

PHOTOGRAPHS

I would like to thank the following people who have given permission to reproduce photographs:

Mr Douglas Spence and the *Dundee Courier and Advertiser* (3, 4, 8, 9, 11, 12, 17, 19, 21)
The National Museum of Antiquities of Scotland (1, 2, 6, 7, 14, 15, 16, 20)

Dundee Public Libraries (5, 10, 13, 18)
Dr. Bruce Walker (20)
Mr Stanley Paget (14)
Baxter Bros. Ltd. (15)
St Andrews University Library (16)
Mr David Kane (21)

Except where otherwise indicated, all songs have been collected and arranged by myself.

Nigel Gatherer.

Contents

Ballads

The term *ballad* is difficult to define. It was originally a song accompanied by a dance (the word *ballet* is still related to this meaning), but now it is used as a general term for a type of folksong which was used to tell a story. In the case of the older classic ballads, the story might be one of a murder of some lord, or relate the tale of some historical or legendary event. In the case of the street ballads, it was often a tale of a local scandal or political protest. Many of the older ballads, which were extensively collected in the nineteenth century, were taken down from oral sources after being passed from generation to generation by oral transmission, whereas street ballads, in the form of broadsides and chapbooks, often originated from printed sources.

Many old ballads and folksongs survive to this day in the mouths of traditional singers, and the folksong revival of the last twenty years has brought about a widespread renewal of interest in this important part of Scotland's folk heritage.

Before literacy was widespread, street balladry was a popular form of entertainment as well as providing the general public with the latest news. The ballad singer would obtain a printed sheet (of which broadsides were one type) and sing to crowds in exchange for money. In Dundee, this tradition could be said to have carried on into the twentieth century, thanks to a shop in the Overgate called the Poets' Box. The shop sold not only ballads, but recitations, speeches and all types of songs. Many of

Prospectus Civitatis TAODUNI ab Oriente. The Prospect of y Town of DUNDEE from y East.

1. Dundee from the east. From Slezer's *Theatrum Scotiae* (1693).

these were hung up and displayed in the window, with thousands more kept in cardboard boxes inside. It was during the hiring fairs, when ploughmen came into Dundee from bothies and farms for miles around, that the Poets' Box was at its busiest, because after the business of getting a fee was complete, the 'bothy cheils' would drink and listen to the latest songs, often paying a literate to sing them. Among the contemporary news stories in song sold by the Poets' Box were 'The Dundee Whale', the story of the famous Tay Whale, and 'The Fall of the Tay Bridge'.

2. The Poets' Box shop in the Overgate. Standing outside is its one-time proprietor, Lowden MacArtney.

1. THE CONSTABLE OF DUNDEE

Moderately

1. Now fortune was false and betrayed a man, He was Constable of Dundee,

And he ween'd that his ae dochter would help him out of his mise - rie.

She was the heiress of her father, — Great Constable of Dundee;

But she would never marry a man, Save ane wha sail'd the sea.

2. 'Oh hold your tongue, my ae dochter, Your folly you'll let be;
Perhaps the sea will be his grave, And drowned he may be.'
'Oh hold your tongue, my good father, Your folly you'll let be;
For none do die, but those that are fey, By the storms of the sea.'

3. Then she was married and brought home To the bonny town of Dundee;
It was by the finest mariner, That ever sail'd the sea.
He hadna sail'd a month, a month, A month, but barely three;
Till he has lost all his ship's goods By the storms of the sea.

4. And then all naked he came home To the bonny town of Dundee;
And he has taken close bedding, And laid him down to dee.
But she is on to her true love, And kiss'd him tenderlie,
'Get up, get up, my own true love, For gear lie not down to dee.'

5. 'For I will on to my father, And an asking he'll grant me;
He'll give me some of his good red goud, To help my love to sea.'
Now she is on to her old father, And fell low down on her knee –
'An asking, an asking, my own father, An asking you'll grant me.'

6. 'Ask on, ask on, my ae dochter, What may your asking be?'
'You'll give me some of your good red goud To help my love to the sea.'
He's turn'd him richt and roun about – A licht, licht laugh gaed he, –
'Drink weel the browst that ye ha'e brewen. Ye'll never get gear frae me.'

3

7. She's risen to her foot again, The saut tear in her ee,
   Says, 'Woe be to your ill won gear, Since you help not my love to the sea!'
   But she has sold both hat and skirt, And mantle tenderlie;
   And she has built a bonny ship And sent her love to the sea.

8. He hadna sail'd a month, a month, A month but barely three;
   Till he has gain'd thrice as much goud As he lost by the storms of the sea.
   And he has built another ship Wi goud and white monie,
   And he has built a bonny ship And sent her to Dundee.

9. And he bade his love drink of the beer, And claret tenderlie, –
   'Drink well the browst that ye ha brewen, Till I come back to thee.'
   When seven years were past and gone, Her father came to poverty,
   And he's done him to his ae dochter, – Fell low down on his knee.

10. 'An asking, an asking, my ae dochter, An asking ye'll grant me.'
    'Ask on, ask on, my old father, What may your asking be?'
    'You'll give some of your good red goud, And some of your white monie,
    You'll give me some of your good red goud, To help me in my misery.'

11. She turn'd her richt an' roun about, 'Tak your ain words,' said she,
    'Drink weel the browst that ye hae brewen, You'll never get gear frae me.'
    He did him to his foot again, The tear blinded his ee;
    'Oh, father,' she said, 'I'll gie you gear, to help you in your misery.'

3. Broughty Castle ('Broughty Wa's').

2. BROUGHTY WA'S

1. Burd Helen was her mother's dear, and her father's heir to be:

He was the laird of Broughty Wa's, and the Provost o' Dundee.

2. Glenhazlen was a comely youth,
   And virtuous were his friends,
   He left the schools o' bonny Dundee
   And on to Aberdeen.

3. It fell upon Christmas day,
   Burd Helen was alone.
   To keep her father's towers,
   They stand two miles from town.

4. Glenhazlen's on to Broughty Wa's,
   Was thinking to win in,
   But the wind it blew and the rain dang on,
   And wat him tae the skin.

5. He was very well entertained
   Baith for his bed and board.
   Till a band o' men surrounded them,
   Weel armed wi spear and sword.

6. They hurried her alang wi them,
   Locked up her maid behind,
   They threw the keys out ower the walls,
   That none their plot might find.

7. They carried her alang wi them,
   Ower many a rocky glen,
   But all that they could say or do,
   From weeping would not refrain.

8. The Hielan Hills are hie hills,
   The Hieland Hills are hie,
   They are no like the banks o' Tay,
   Or the bonny toon o' Dundee.

9. One day when they were walking
   And for to take the air,
   She threw herself into the stream
   Against wind and despair.

10. It was sae deep he couldna wide,
    Boats were nae to be found,
    He threw himself in after her,
    And sank down like a stone.

11. She kilted up her green claiding,
    A little below her knee,
    And never rest nor was undressed
    Till she reached again Dundee.

12. 'I learned this at Broughty Wa's,
    At Broughty near Dundee.
    If water was my prison deep,
    I'd swim for liberty.'

3. BONNIE ANNIE LIVIESTON

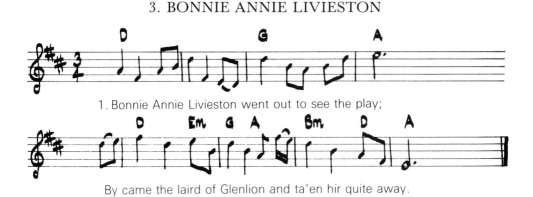

1. Bonnie Annie Livieston went out to see the play;

By came the laird of Glenlion and ta'en hir quite away.

2. He set hir on a milk-white steed, Himself upon a gray;
   He's ta'en hir o'er the Highland hills And ta'en hir quite away.

3. When they came to Glenlion's gate They lighted on the green;
   There was mony a bonny lad and lass To welcome the lady hame.

4. They led hir through high towers and bowers And through the buling-green,
   And aye when they spake Erse to hir The tears blinded hir een.

5. Says, The Highlands is no for me, kind sir, The Highlands is no for me,
   If that ye would my favour win Take me unto Dundee.

6. Dundee, he says, Dundee, lady – Dundee you shall never see;
   Upon the laird of Glenlion soon wadded shall ye be.

7. When bells were rung and mass was sung And all were bound for bed,
   And bonny Anny Livieston By hir bridegroom was laid;

8. It's O gin it were day, she says, It's O gin it were day;
O if that it were day, she says, Nae langer wad I stay.

9. Your horse stands in a good stable Eating both corn and hay,
And you are in Glenlion's arms; Why should ye weary for day?

10. Glenlion's arms are good enough, But alais, they're no for me;
If that you would my favour win take me unto Dundee.

11. Bat fetch me paper, pen and ink, And candle that I may see;
And I'll go write a long letter to Geordie in Dundee.

12. Where will I get a bonny boy That will win horse and shoon,
That will gang to my ain true-luve And tell him what is done?

13. Then up spake a bonny boy Near to Glenlion's kin;
Says, Many time I hae gane his errand, But the lady's I will rin.

14. O when he came to broken brigs He bent his bow and swame,
And when he came to grass growing Set down his feet and ran.

15. And when he came to Dundee gate Lap clean out o'er the wa';
Before the porter was thereat The boy was in the ha'.

16. What news, what news, bonny boy? What news has thou to me?
No news, no news, said bonny boy, But a letter unto thee.

17. The first three lines he looked on, A loud laughter gied he;
But or he wan to the hinder en The tears blinded his ee.

18. Gae saddle tae me the black, he says, Gae saddle tae me the broun;
Gae saddle tae me the swiftest steed that e'er took man to towen,

19. He burst the black unto the slack, the Broun unto the brae,
But fair fa' on the siller-gray That carried him ay away.

20. When he came to Glenlion's gate He tirled at the pin,
But before that he wan up the stair The lady she was gone.

21. O I can kiss thy cheeks, Anny, O I can kiss thy chin;
O I can kiss thy clay-cold lips Though there be no breath within.

22. Deal large at my love's buriell The short bread and the wine,
And gin the morn at ten o'clock Ye may deal as muckle at mine.

23. The taen was buried in Mary's kirk, The tither in St. Mary's quire,
And out of the taen there grew a birk, And the ither a bonny brier.

24. And ay they grew, and ay they threw, Till they did meet aboon;
And a' that e'er the same did see Knew they had true lovers been.

4. THERE CAM A LADDIE FRAE THE NORTH

Sung to the tune of 'Bonnie Annie Livieston' (No. 3)

1. There cam a laddie frae the north,
   Wi courage frank and free;
   And he's fa'en in love wi a bonnie lass
   That lived into Dundee.

2. 'What aileth thee, my bonnie lass,
   That the saut tear blin's your ee?'
   'O haud your tongue, young man,' she said,
   'And dinna scorn me.'

3. 'Dinna ye mind, young man,' she said,
   'When sportin we hae been,
   Ye promised for to marry me,
   And frae shame ye wad me screen?'

4. 'And sae I will, my bonnie lass,
   Ere mony months gae by,
   I will come back and marry you
   And tak ye to Strathspey.'

5. 'The Hielan hills are very high,
   And O, they're ill to clim,
   And I fear if ance ye get owre them
   Ye'll no come back again.

6. 'Besides, your father he will fret,
   Your mither she will frown,
   Your sisters they will say to me,
   Gae hame, ye lowland dame.'

7. 'Ye dread say muckle ill o' me,
   I fear ye'll smell the rue;
   And if ye slight my parents dear,
   I will bid you adieu.'

8. He's taen his pikestaff in his hand,
   His kilt abeen his knee;
   Says 'Fare ye-weel, my bonnie lass,
   For ye'll get nae mair o' me.'

9. He's gane hame to his mither,
   But nae sleep could wink his ee
   For thinkin o' the bonnie lass
   He left into Dundee.

10. 'What aileth thee, my only son?
    Ye've lost your mirth and glee;
    I fear your heart it is not here,
    Ye've left it in Dundee.

11. 'Ye'll tak your pikestaff in your hand,
    Wi' your kilt abeen your knee;
    It's only like three score o' mile
    Until ye cross the Dee.'

12. He's put on his Sunday coat,
    Wi' his kilt abeen his knee,
    And he's taen the lassie by the hand
    That he left in Dundee.

13. Kissin's good in Februar',
    And clappin's good in May;
    But I hae married my bonnie lass,
    And ta'en her to Strathspey.

5. BONNIE SUSIE CLELAND

1. There lived a lady in Scotland, Hey my love and ho my jo, There lived a lady in Scotland, And dearly she loved me, There lived a lady in Scotland, And she's fa'n in love wi an English-man, And bonnie Susie Cleland is tae be burnt in Dun-dee.

9

2. The father untae the dochter cam,
     Hey my love and ho my jo,
   The father untae the dochter cam,
     And dearly she loved me,
   The father untae the dochter cam,
   Sayin, 'Will you forsake that Englishman?'
     And bonnie Susie Cleland is tae be burnt in Dundee.

3. 'If you'll no that Englishman forsake,
     So dearly loved by thee,
   It's I will burn you at the stake.'

4. 'I'll no that Englishman forsake,
     Who dearly loveth me,
   Though you may burn me at the stake.'

5. Oh where will I get a pretty little boy,
     That dearly loveth me,
   Who'll carry tidings to my joy.

6. Oh here I am a pretty little boy,
     Who dearly loveth thee,
   Who'll carry tidings tae thy joy.

7. Oh gie tae him this richt hand glove,
     That dearly loveth me,
   Tell him tae get another love.

8. Gie tae him this wee penknife,
     That dearly loveth me,
   Tell him tae get another wife.

9. And gie tae him this gey gold ring,
     Who dearly loveth me,
   Say, 'I am going tae ma burning.'

10. Her father he ca'd up the stake,
      Hey my love and ho my jo,
    Her father he ca'd up the stake,
      That dearly loveth me,
    Her father he ca'd up the stake,
    Her brither he the fire did make,
      And bonnie Susie Cleland she was burnt in Dundee.

As sung by Jim Reid, Dundee
Arranged by Peter Shepheard

6. THE SKIPPER O' DUNDEE

Drearily

1. The skipper brocht his guid ship hame, And he anchored aff the toun;
And he wondered hoo a' the bells were ringin, As he walked up an' doon,
And he said, "I've been gane for mony a year, And in mony cities been;
And I wadnae gie for this auld toon, The grandest I hae seen."

2. And I hae seen fowk braw and bauld,
   And ladies fair an' a';
   But mair I think o' ma mither auld,
   That wons in Thorter Row.
   But aye the skipper heard the bells,
   And the noise o' shoutin loud,
   As gin a' the people in the toun,
   Were gaithered in a crowd.

3. And he saw abeen the market place,
   A reek and whiles a bleeze;
   The skipper wistna what it was,
   But his hert was ill at ease.
   At length cam oot the harbour boat,
   Should hae been oot lang before;
   'Now tell us quickly harbour fowk,
   What's a' the steer ashore?'

4. A baillie auld sat in the boat,
   And sternly he did say,
   'We hae been burnin o' a witch
   Weel kent as Janet Grey.'
   Oh ghastly grew the skipper's look,
   And he cried, 'Aloud ye lee,
   I'll tak the truth frae Weelum Greig,
   That gae tae schule wi me.

5. I'll take the truth frae Weelum Greig,
   That pu's the foremost oar;
   Oh tell the truth now Weelum Greig,
   If e'er ye spak't afore.'
   Then up an' answered Weelum Greig,
   'Would it were false the which;
   This very hour yer mither auld,
   Was burnt for a witch.'

6. The skipper grippit the taffrail hard,
   While sicht an' sound grew dim;
   And a' the bonnie country showed
   In blood red hues tae him.
   The skipper warsled sair wi grief,
   An' a wecht lay on his breist;
   An' helplessly he turned his heid,
   And looked frae west tae east.

7. He looked upon the ripplin tide,
   An' a boat that rockin lay;
   An' said, 'Now let there be a curse
   Upon the river Tay.
   And upon a' within that wa,
   My curse fa late or soon;
   Aye heavy fa the wrath of God,
   Upon this bloody toun.'

8. 'Let their reward be the sharp-edged sword,
   Let it fa on first and least;
   Frae the auld man wi the straw white pow,
   Tae the baby at the breist.'
   He turned him to his trusty crew,
   An' motioned wi his hand,
   They raised the anchor an pu'd the ropes,
   An' the ship turned frae the land.

9. They gaed oot fairly wi the tide,
   An' doon the river free;
   An' never to return again
   Tae their home toun o' Dundee.

Words old, tune composed by Jim Reid.
As sung by Jim Reid, arranged by Peter Shepheard.

12

7. THE BANKS OF SWEET DUNDEE I

1. Young William was a ploughboy, his fate to you I will unfold, He was sent

from his Mary for the sake of cursed gold He was torn from his Mary, and

sent to plough the sea; While she lamented sorely on the banks of

sweet Dundee. But fortune smil'd on William as he was on the raging main;

Yet still the thoughts of Mary oft fill'd his mind with pain, Since for the

sake of her he lov'd he was sent o'er the sea, To plough the briny ocean

from the banks of sweet Dundee.

2. Young William from the foretop a strange sail did chance to spy,
The captain view'd her and did say, 'I think she does lay by;
Come clear the deck for action, my heroes bold and free!'
Then William thought of Mary and the banks of sweet Dundee.
The bloody battle then began, the fiery cannon loud did roar:
And many a wounded seaman lay bleeding in his gore;
Young William by a musket shot was wounded in the knee;
And as he fell he cried, 'Farewell to the banks of sweet Dundee!'

3. At length she struck her colours, and then with victory they were crown'd,
   And freighted with great riches, to England they were bound;
   When they arrived in England, each man was paid so free;
   Then William sought his Mary on the banks of sweet Dundee.
   When he arriv'd at sweet Dundee, he met his Mary all alone,
   And said, 'My pretty maiden, why do you sigh and mourn?'
   She said, 'It's for my William that was banish'd far from me,
   And sent across the ocean from the banks of sweet Dundee.'

4. 'If William was your lover's name, I knew that young man very well;
   When boarding of a Spanish ship, 'twas then your William fell;
   And as he lay in grief and pain, these words he said to me –
   'Tell Mary I shall ne'er return to the banks of sweet Dundee.'
   When this she heard, she down did fall, and gave a loud and bitter cry –
   'If William's dead, with broken heart I'll wander till I die!
   It's cursed gold has caused all my grief and misery,
   And left me broken hearted on the banks of sweet Dundee.'

5. He said, 'My Mary, you are true, I am your William come again,
   That was sent from his Mary to plough the raging main;
   But though sent from you, my sweet love, I ever thought of thee,
   When lying wounded far from thee, and the banks of sweet Dundee.
   Then dry thy tears, my Mary, and think no more of grief and pain,
   Since I'm returned with gold in store to sweet Dundee again:
   For to the sea I'll bid adieu, and we'll now happy be,
   And we will soon get married on the banks of sweet Dundee.'

8. THE ROON-MOO'ED SPADE

1. Geordie Mill wi' his roon moo'ed spade Is wishin' aye for mair fouk deid, For the sake o' the donnal an' the bit shortbread, When he gangs wi' the spaiks i' the mornin'. An' if the tale that's tauld be true, A greater gain he has in view, Which mak's his fry-ing pan richt fu' To skirl baith nicht an' mornin'.

2. A porter cam to Geordie's door,
   A hairy trunk on his back he bore,
   Which the Quentin Durward frae Leith shore
   Brought roond that very morning.
   This trunk, I'm tauld, contained a line,
   Wi sovereigns to the amount of nine,
   The price o' a weel-fed sonsie quine
   They had sent to Munro ae mornin.

3. But Geordie to conceal their plan,
   A story tauld as false as lang,
   Saying the trunk belonged to a travellin man,
   That wad call for it next mornin.
   No Geordie doon to Robbie goes,
   The doctor's line to him he shows,
   Which wished frae them a double dose,
   By the coach on Wednesday mornin.

4. Says Robbie, 'Is the box come back?'
'Oh, yes' says Geordie, giein' the purse a shak,
'An' we maun gae an' no be slack
To fill't again ere mornin.'
Quo' Robbie's wife: 'Oh sirs tak tent,
For sure a warnin' I've been sent,
Which tells me ye will yet repent
Yer conduct on some mornin.'

5. 'Ye fool,' quo' Robbie, 'hush yer fears,
While I've the keys fat deil can steer's?
We've been weel paid for't ten past years,
Think o' auchteen pounds i' the mornin.'
Sae aff they set to Tam and Jock,
The lads that used the spade an' pock,
An' wi Glenarf their throats did soak
To keep them brisk till mornin.

6. The hour grew late, the tryst was lain,
Amang these Resurrection men,
When each his glass did freely drain,
Sayin, 'Here's success to the mornin.'
But Robbie noo does sair repent
His slightin o' the warning sent,
For the noise o' a second coffin's rent
Caused in Dundee a deil o' a mornin.

9. THE WIFE O' DENSIDE

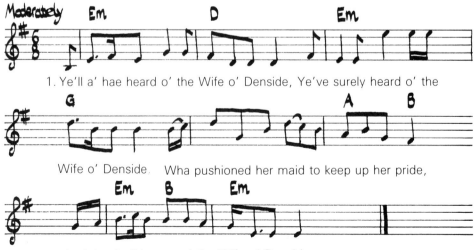

1. Ye'll a' hae heard o' the Wife o' Denside, Ye've surely heard o' the
Wife o' Denside, Wha pushioned her maid to keep up her pride,
And the devil is sure o' the Wife o' Denside.

16

2. The Wife o' Denside, the little wee buddie,
   She tried to tak up the trade o' the howdie,
   But ah! ha, ha! her skill was but sma,
   For she pushioned lassie and bairnie an' a'.

3. Her tippet was brown and her veil it was black,
   An' three lang feathers hung ower her back,
   Wi her purse by her side fu o' guineas sae free,
   That saved her frae death at the Cross o' Dundee.

4. Oh Jeffrey, oh, Jeffrey, ye hinna dune fair,
   For ye've robbed the gallows o' its lawfu heir.
   An' it hadna been you an' your great muckle fee,
   She'd hae hung like a trout at the Cross o' Dundee.

1. THE CONSTABLE OF DUNDEE

In 1298 Alexander Carron was given a charter from Sir William Wallace of some land near Dundee, as well as the office of Constable of Dundee. Carron got the name *Skirmschur* (a sharp fighter) and the Constabulary by an act of bravery in which he subdued an English garrison besieged in Dundee Castle. Dudhope Castle became the home of the Scrymgeours, as they later became, and the office of Constable became hereditary. It would appear that the reign of the Scrymgeours as custodians of Dudhope and of the Constabulary lasted until John Graham of Claverhouse acquired both in 1684. The name Scrymgeour has remained active in Dundee's history, and 'Neddy' Scrymgeour was a prominent Dundee politician in the first half of the twentieth century.

The ballad was collected by William Christie in the 1860s. He noted it from an 80-year-old Banffshire woman who remembered her grandfather singing it, indicating that it is probably of some antiquity.

2. BROUGHTY WA'S

The text is from Child 258.

'Broughty Wa's' refers to the walls of Broughty Castle in Broughty Ferry, Dundee. The castle was built about 1490 and occupied a strategic position commanding the Tay. During its long history it has changed hands between Scots and English, Protestants and Catholics. It fell into disrepair, was restored in 1861, and is now used as the Dundee Whaling Museum.

The ballad tells the story of Helen, the daughter of a provost of Dundee, who is kidnapped and taken north. At one time, men from the Highlands not only reived Lowland sheep and cattle, but also stole women. As Francis J. Child wrote, 'the kidnapping of women for compulsory marriage was a practice which

17

prevailed for hundreds of years'. Other Scottish ballads with similar abduction themes are 'Eppie Morrie', 'Rob Roy' and 'The Lady of Arngask'.

Jim Reid, the Dundee folksinger, sings this ballad to a variant of the tune generally used for 'The Banks of Sweet Dundee'; however, Frank Kidson noted an air called 'Broughty Wa's' from a Mrs Harris, in the manuscript in the Mitchell Library, Glasgow. The 'Child Number' is the number given by Francis Child in his mammoth collection of ballads, *The English and Scottish Popular Ballads* (1882-98), reprinted in 1965 by Dover Publications Ltd.

3. BONNIE ANNIE LIVIESTON

Child No. 222. Tune from the Sharpe MS.

This ballad, also called 'Bonny Baby Livingstone', is quite similar in theme to 'Broughty Wa's'. Bonnie Annie is captured by Glenlion and taken to the Highlands. Glenlion offers her all his flocks and herds for one kind look. She replies:

> O ae kind look ye ne'er shall get,
> Nor win a smile from me,
> Unless to me you'll favour show
> And take me to Dundee.

> Dundee, Baby? Dundee, Baby?
> Dundee you ne'er shall see,
> Till I've carried you to Glenlion
> And have my bride made thee.

Bonnie Annie finds a 'bonny boy' to carry a message to her lover in Dundee. This image is a frequent occurrence in ballads, and verse fourteen is of a type which appears in many English and Scottish ballads. Another verse which is often found is 'Gae saddle tae me the black, the black, Gae saddle tae me the brown' (verse eighteen), which is found in 'The Gypsy Laddies' amongst others.

'Mary's Kirk', mentioned in verse twenty-three, is possibly the church of St Mary, which was erected in Dundee in about 1196 by the Earl of Huntingdon. All that remains of the structure is the church tower, or The Auld Steeple as it is called, in the centre of Dundee.

4. THERE CAM A LADDIE FRAE THE NORTH

From Ord's *Bothy Ballads* (1930). Sung to the tune of 'Bonny Baby Livieston'.

This ballad has many similarities to the previous one. Verse five has the familiar 'The Heilan' hills are very high', echoed in both 'Broughty Wa's' and 'Baby Livieston', but the story of this ballad is more to do with a lovers' tiff than the terrible consequences of the other two.

5. BONNIE SUSIE CLELAND

As sung by Jim Reid, recorded by Peter Shepheard.

This a version of the ballad 'Lady Maisry' (Child 65), and it was originally collected by William Motherwell.

6. THE SKIPPER O' DUNDEE

Words old, tune composed by Jim Reid. Recorded from Jim Reid by Peter Shepheard.

In *The Bards of Angus and the Mearns,* it says of this ballad: '. . . This ballad is founded on a true incident in local history. The burning of Grizzel Jeffrey for alleged witchcraft at the Cross of Dundee happened in the days so discreditable to our Scottish intelligence and humanity'. The source is given as a volume of poetry called *Poems by Two,* printed by D. R. Clark and Sons, Dundee in 1882.

7. THE BANKS OF SWEET DUNDEE I

William Christie noted the air and words from 'a native of Aberdeenshire' in 1850 for his *Traditional Ballad Airs* (1876). He added that '. . . copies of the ballad are found in different forms in chap-books and broadsides, all having different versions of the story'. It is likely that the ballad of the same name (No. 57) is the subject of the versions alluded to.

This ballad is very similar to 'The Plains of Waterloo', and although it does not mention a love token, it uses the same device of the long away lover testing his sweetheart's love.

8. THE ROON MOO'ED SPADE

The tune is 'Hey Johnnie Cope', and the text is from *Haunted Dundee* by A. H. Millar (1923).

The Anatomy Act of 1832 gave medical schools the opportunity of legitimately acquiring bodies for dissection, but before that, many anatomy professors were less than fussy about where the bodies came from. Stories of the Resurrectionists, the men who robbed graves for bodies, were common, and some Resurrectionists found easier ways of supplying corpses. In Edinburgh during the 1820s two Irish labourers, Burke and Hare, shocked the city when it was discovered that they had been murdering innocent passers-by and delivering their bodies to Robert Knox at Edinburgh University.

In Scotland, sextons were often suspected of body-snatching. Geordie Mill was the sexton in charge of the Auld Howff, the oldest burial place in Dundee, and such was the suspicion of his being a Resurrectionist that watches were set up at the Howff to catch him in the act. This came to nothing, but William McNab (b. 1789), a neighbour of Mill's and the instigator of much of the suspicion, wrote a song called 'The Roon Moo'ed Spade' which was quite direct in accusing the sexton of supplying bodies to the medical school in Edinburgh.

The song was evidently very popular in Dundee as a street ballad, and probably led to the suspension of George Mill from his duties, after which he began weaving for a living. Attempts to bring charges against McNab, who was at that time a precentor of St Mary's Church, Dundee came to nothing, and he wrote another song called 'A Lamentation for the Loss of the Roon Moo'ed Spade'. The song makes mention of 'he wha leads the auld kirk ban'' (McNab), who 'filled the toon fu' o' a sang That's dwined me o' my spade'. The round-mouthed spade was the tool used to dig the graves, and a symbol of the position of sexton.

9. THE WIFE O' DENSIDE

Local murder stories like 'The Wife of Denside' were great material for the broadside writers. The Smith family, i.e. Mrs Smith (The Wife of Denside) and her two sons, lived at the farm of Denside, near Broughty Ferry, with three maid-servants. One of the servants, Margaret Walden, was cast out because she had an illegitimate child, but she was later allowed to return. George Smith, one of the sons, fell in love with her, which caused another row when she became pregnant again. Mrs Smith gave Margaret various potions in an attempt to bring about an abortion, but the servant died on 8th September 1826. After her body was exhumed some time later, it was proved that she had died of arsenic poisoning, and that Mrs Smith had bought arsenic previous to the servant's death. Whether she had committed suicide, as she had talked about, or been accidentally killed during the attempted abortion, or had been murdered, was the subject of a lengthy trial at which the Wife of Denside was tried for murder. The verdict returned was 'not proven', a unique Scottish verdict meaning neither guilty nor innocent, but the public of Dundee still believed that Mrs Smith was a murderess.

This is an old song, published in A. H. Millar's *Haunted Dundee*. The tune is 'The Laird o' Cockpen', and the first verse gave rise to another murder song, 'The Wife o' Gateside'.

The history of Scotland in the seventeenth century is very much about the struggle between Episcopacy (the Church ruled by bishops appointed by the king) and Presbyterianism (the Church ruled by ministers and elders chosen by the congregation). The Stuart kings endorsed Episcopalianism, but the Reformation had taken a strong hold in Scotland, and as the monarchs were to find out, it was not an easy thing to persuade the country to abolish the Presbytery.

Charles I tried to force Scotland to accept Episcopacy, but the Presbyterians took action to protect their religion. In 1638 the National Covenant was drawn up and thousands of Scots pledged their lives to the defence of the Presbytery. The Covenanters joined forces with the English puritans in ousting Charles, but under Cromwell's rule the Scots suffered at the hands of the English yet again. Cromwell was determined to make Scotland part of England, and he appointed General Monck as commander of Scotland. Monck captured many towns and established garrisons there.

Dundee was at this time one of the most strongly fortified towns in Scotland, and one of the richest. Monck had encountered very little resistance from the towns he had entered previously, but when he marched to Dundee he found the town virtually impregnable and armed with 10,000 men. Because of the superb fortification, refugees driven out of Edinburgh, Glasgow and Perth had removed themselves and their valuables to Dundee. Monck realised the importance of the town and proceeded to lay siege. After six weeks the English managed to enter, and there followed scenes of massacre which reputedly lasted for three days.

After Cromwell's death both the Scots and the English were keen to reinstate Charles II, but his welcome was to be short-lived. He ordered the Covenant to be burned in public and again tried to establish Episcopacy in Scotland. The Presbyterians were persecuted and forced to meet in secret.

Charles died in 1685 and was succeeded by James II, who continued the persecution of Covenanters with such ferocity that the period was called 'the killing time'. King James put John Graham of Claverhouse in charge of a body of troops, and for many years Claverhouse was notorious for the severity and zeal with which he ruthlessly hounded the Covenanters.

Bonnie Dundee

More than any other, John Graham of Claverhouse emerges as a figure of great historical significance from Dundee's past. His loyalty to James

4. Dudhope Castle, home of Claverhouse.

matched his hostility to the Covenant, and both were legendary. His merciless persecution of the Presbyterians earned him the nicknames of 'Bloody Claver'se' and 'the De'il'. On the other hand, his supporters dubbed him 'Bonnie Dundee' and 'Iain Dubh nan Cath' (Black John of the Battles).

John Graham was born at Claverhouse, north of Dundee in the 1640s, and was educated at St. Andrews. In about 1672 he enrolled in a Scottish regiment serving in France and then went to Holland where, ironically, he saved the life of the young Prince William of Orange. In 1677 he returned to Scotland where a year later he was given command of a regiment of horse. For the next few years his activities in the south and south-west of Scotland gave him his disagreeable reputation for cruelty. Stories of cold-blooded murder and massacre are common.

Graham's rewards for his loyalty and services to the king were considerable. He was made Viscount Dundee, and was given the Castle of Dudhope near Dundee and the Constabulary of Dundee.

5. John Graham of Claverhouse (1648-89).

10. THE BONNETS OF BONNIE DUNDEE

1. To the Lords of Convention 'twas Claverhouse spoke, Ere the King's
crown go down there are crowns to be broke; So each Cavalier who loves
honour and me, Let him follow the bonnets of Bonnie Dundee.

CHORUS: Come fill up my cup, come fill up my can, Come saddle my horses and
call out my men, Unhook the West Port, and let us go free,
For it's up with the bonnets of Bonnie Dundee.

2. Dundee he is mounted, he rides up the street,
   The bells they ring backward, the drums they are beat,
   But the Provost (douce man) said, 'Just e'en let it be,
   For the town is weel rid o' that deil o' Dundee'.

3. There are hills beyond Pentland, and lands beyond Forth,
   If there's Lords in the South, there are Chiefs in the North,
   There are brave Duinewassals, three thousand times three,
   Will cry 'Hey for the bonnets of Bonnie Dundee!'

4. Then away to the hills, to the caves, to the rocks,
   Ere I own a usurper I'll couch with the fox;
   And tremble, false Whigs, in the midst of your glee,
   Ye have not seen the last o' my bonnets and me!'

24

11. KILLIECRANKIE

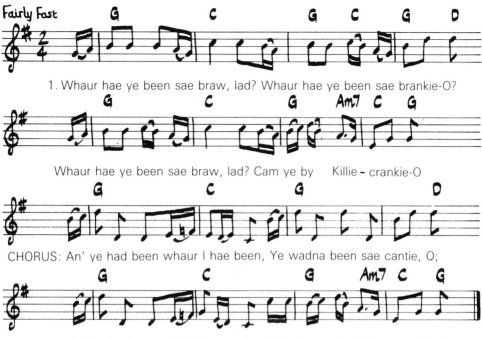

1. Whaur hae ye been sae braw, lad? Whaur hae ye been sae brankie-O?

Whaur hae ye been sae braw, lad? Cam ye by Killie-crankie-O

CHORUS: An' ye had been whaur I hae been, Ye wadna been sae cantie, O;

An' ye had seen what I hae seen, I' the braes o' Killie-crankie, O.

2. I fought at land, I fought at sea,
   At hame I fought my auntie, O;
   But I met the devil and Dundee
   On the braes o' Killiecrankie, O.

3. The bauld Pitcur fell in a furr,
   And Clavers gat a clankie, O,
   Or I had fed an Athol gled
   On the braes o' Killiecrankie, O.

4. Oh, fie, Mackay! what gart ye lie
   I' the bush ayont the brankie, O;
   Ye'd better kiss'd King Willie's loof,
   Than come to Killiecrankie, O.

   Final Chorus:
   It's nae shame, it's nae shame,
   It's nae shame tae shank ye, O;
   There's sour slaes on Athol braes,
   And deils at Killiecrankie, O.

12. LADY DUNDEE'S LAMENT

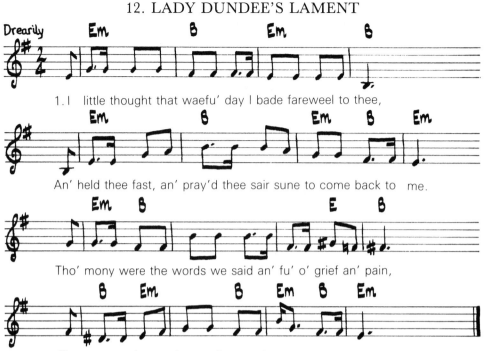

Drearily

1. I little thought that waefu' day I bade fareweel to thee,
An' held thee fast, an' pray'd thee sair sune to come back to me.
Tho' mony were the words we said an' fu' o' grief an' pain,
They were to be our last, an' we sud never meet again.

2. 'Mourn not,' thou said'st; 'ye ken my faith
Is given but to three,
Unstained I keep it to my king,
My country an' to thee.
As cauld as ice, as hard as steel
I gang among them a';
An' my heart's wi thee at Dudhope,
When I am far awa'.'

3. Thy spirit was the gentlest, but
Where duty led it on,
Thou did'st neither shrink nor falter,
Till the rugged way was won.
Fause were the words they said of thee,
They called thee harsh and stern,
They kenned na how the heart was wrung
That wad neither flinch nor turn.

4. They might hae kenned the bitter signs,
They were na far to seek,
In the sadness o' thy glorious ee,
The paleness o' thy cheek.
A stormy life, a hero's death,
An' deathless fame are thine;
When a' thy foes forgotten lie
The clearer will it shine.

5. The mools are on the gallant heart
   That aye beat true to me;
   The dust lies ower the waving hair,
   I never mair shall see.
   The ringing voice is silent,
   That echoed wild and free,
   An' stirred the blude o' auld and young
   Wi the war-cry o' 'Dundee'.

13. THE PIPER O' DUNDEE

1. The piper cam' tae oor toon, Tae oor toon, tae oor toon, The piper cam' tae oor toon, And he played bonni-lie: He played a spring the laird to please, A spring brent new frae 'yont the seas, And then he ga'e the bags a squeeze, And played a-nither key. CHORUS: And wasna he a roguey, A roguey, a roguey? And wasna he a roguey, The Piper o' Dundee.

2. He played 'The Welcome Ower the Main',
   And 'Ye'se be Fou and I'se be Fain',
   And 'Auld Stuart's Back Again',
   Wi muckle mirth and glee;
   He played 'The Kirk', he played 'The Quier',
   'The Mullin Dhu', and 'Chevalier',
   And 'Lang Awa' but Welcome Here',
   Sae sweet, sae bonnilie.

3. It's some gat swords, and some gat nane,
   And some were dancing mad their lane,
   And mony a vow o' weir was ta'en,
   That nicht at Amulrie!
   There was Tullibardine and Burleigh,
   And Struan, Keith and Ogilvie,
   And brave Carnegie, wha but he,
   The Piper o' Dundee?

14. THE TAY BRIDGE DISASTER

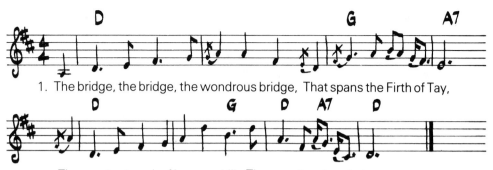

1. The bridge, the bridge, the wondrous bridge, That spans the Firth of Tay,

The greatest work of human skill, The wonder of each day.

2. Its lofty pillars stood erect,
   And bore its girders high,
   A noble sight when underneath,
   Great ships went sailing by.

3. A glory to the world it stood,
   And a glory to Dundee,
   An iron bridge so strongly built,
   Across the raging sea.

4. But what's the strength of bolt and bar,
   And what's the skill of man,
   Compared with nature's blast that blows,
   Produced by nature's fan.

5. How large and strong the beams may be,
   That stretch across the span,
   But let the tempest breathe its blast,
   And iron yields like wands.

6. 'Twas Sabbath eve the train had left,
   Old Scotland's chiefest town,
   Where stands the holy Holyrood,
   A palace of renown.

7. From stage to stage the train speeds on,
   And quickly wends its way,
   Through hill and dale and country vale,
   Bound for the banks of Tay.

8. Its living freight of young and old,
   It gathered by the way,
   Some were fearful some were bold,
   And some were glad and gay.

9. Some sad at heart their way direct,
   The sick to tend and cheer,
   While others with their friends expect,
   To spend a guid New Year.

10. A father with his children sits,
    The youngest in his arms,
    A smile of joy upon his lips,
    He never thinks of harm.

11. A youth in manhood prime is seen,
    A maid sits by his side,
    The object of his love so keen,
    About to be his bride.

12. The train speeds on its fatal course,
    And nears the spot of doom,
    The bridge is seen while passing clouds,
    Unveiled the pale faced moon.

13. Amidst the tempest loudest blast,
    The train it did proceed,
    When Ah! no human hand or skill,
    Could stay the fatal deed.

14. The train into the girders came,
    And loud the winds did roar,
    A flash is seen, the bridge is down,
    The train is heard no more.

15. The bridge is down the bridge is down,
    The word in terror spread,
    The train is gone, its living freight
    Lie mingled with the dead.

16. Twas sad to see the open gap,
    At morrow's light of day,
    But sadder still to think of those,
    That perished in the Tay.

17. But what is life a thread of breath,
    That's easy snatched away,
    We are in life so near to death,
    It's taught us day by day.

18. Dry up your tears ye friends that weep,
    And lean upon the Lord,
    The widow's stay be the orphan's friend,
    It's taught us in His Word.

As sung by Mrs Balfour, Lindores, Fife.
Collected and arranged by Peter Shepheard.

6. The first Tay rail bridge before the disaster in 1879.

10. THE BONNETS OF BONNIE DUNDEE

Four verses from a longer song in Scott's *The Doom of Devorgoil,* a melodrama written for the Adelphi Theatre, Edinburgh.

The chorus was based on the chorus of 'Jockey's Escape from Dundee' (No. 28), which also may have been taken from an earlier source. The tune was called 'The Band at a Distance', and was used as a march by military bands. At Bannockburn in 1314, a body of men representing the town of Dundee styled themselves 'the bonnets of bonnie Dundee', which may have inspired Scott to give that name to the followers of Claverhouse. However, the song is about a particular incident that happened in Edinburgh in 1689.

During the 1680s, Edinburgh had been filling up with supporters of the Presbyterian Prince William of Orange, and opposition to King James was strongly felt in Scotland. In England in 1688, a Convention ruled that James, now an expatriate, had abdicated. Prince William ordered a similar Convention in Edinburgh, and it was only a matter of time before James lost the Scottish crown as well.

Claverhouse, still loyal to James, did everything he could to disrupt the Convention and delay the fall of the king. After hearing that some Covenanters were planning to assassinate him, however, he realised that Edinburgh was no longer a safe place for a man of his reputation and sympathies. He galloped through the city with a troop of fifty horsemen, and when asked where he was going he replied, 'Wherever the spirit of Montrose shall direct me.' Montrose had originally been sympathetic to the Covenant, but had latterly fought for the king.

Crowds gathered round the horsemen, now at one of the gates of the city, the West Port, and for a while the Lords of the Convention were under the impression that Viscount Dundee was at the gates of the city with an army, ready to invade.

In spite of the hatred for Claverhouse, there is no doubt that he commanded great respect and fear, as Scott's song illustrates:

> With sour-faced Whigs the Grassmarket was cramm'd,
> As if half the West had set tryst to be hang'd;
> There was spite in each look, there was fear in each e'e,
> As they watched for the bonnets o' Bonnie Dundee.

> These cowls of Kilmarnock had spits and had spears,
> And lang-hafted gullies to kill Cavaliers:
> But they shrunk to close-heads, and the causeway was free,
> At the toss of the bonnet o' Bonnie Dundee.

Claverhouse left Edinburgh and headed for the North, where he gathered together an army of Highlanders.

In April 1689 the Lords of Convention ruled that James had 'forfaulted' his right to the throne by being a 'professed Papist' and that 'The throne was become vacant'. William was proclaimed king the next day.

11. KILLIECRANKIE

From James Hogg's *Jacobite Relics of Scotland* (1819-21).

For a number of weeks Claverhouse and his Highland army carried out a series of guerilla attacks against William's government. One of these incidents involved the setting of the Hilltown in Dundee ablaze after being frustrated in trying to enter the town. In 1684 Claverhouse had been appointed Constable of Dundee, and in 1688 he was made Provost of the town, which was supposed to make him 'absolute'. The Magistrates were never on good terms with Claverhouse, and argued with him about his jurisdiction, so it was for revenge that he set out for Dundee with the intention of causing destruction. So much against Claverhouse were the Magistrates that soon after Dundee became a rallying point for his adversary, General Mackay.

General Mackay was in charge of Dutch regiments in Scotland with the purpose of putting an end to the activities of Claverhouse. In July 1689 they reached the pass of Killiecrankie in Perthshire, where Mackay noticed that Dundee and his army were waiting, and he realised that he was trapped.

The Highlanders were more used to the steep ground than the Dutchmen trained in the Low Countries, but Mackay's army outnumbered Dundee's by about 4,000 to 2,500. The armies faced each other for more than two hours while Claverhouse waited for the sun to disappear over the mountain tops. Then he gave the order to charge.

The battle was won by Dundee's troops, Mackay having lost more than 2,000 men, but Dundee himself was shot and killed. It had been said many years before that Dundee was in league with the Devil, and that he could only be killed with a silver bullet, and there is a legend that at Killiecrankie he was shot by a silver button. However, despite the victory, Dundee's army had lost the dynamic leadership which had given them so much power, and the initial success turned into a strategic defeat when the army dispersed. King William, when asked to send reinforcements to Scotland, said, '. . . armies are needless: the war is over with Dundee's life'.

12. LADY DUNDEE'S LAMENT

'The Lament of Lady Dundee' was written by Lady John Scott (previously Alicia Ann Spottiswoode), and in her lyric she shows a certain sympathy for Viscount Dundee's cause. As a member of an aristocratic family Lady Scott perhaps grew up in an atmosphere of loyalty to the rightful king, but her main sympathy lies with the bereaved Lady Dundee at Dudhope.

The woman Claverhouse chose for his wife was Jean Cochrane, the daughter of Lord Cochrane of the house of Dundonald in Ayrshire. They were married in 1684, the year Claverhouse acquired the lordship of Dudhope. There was a lot of controversy surrounding the marriage, as opposition stemmed from both sides. Jean Cochrane's mother was an ardent supporter of the Covenant, and her grandfather, the Earl of Dundonald, was threatened with prosecution for harbouring fugitives. They naturally abhorred the match with 'Bloody Claver'se', the scourge of the Covenanters, and many of the Royalists and friends of Claverhouse were suspicious and uneasy about the marriage into a Covenanting family. He answered his critics by saying that '. . . it is not in the power of love nor any other folly to alter my loyalty', and that 'I may cure people of that plaigue of presbitry . . . but cannot be infected . . . For the young lady herself, I shall answer for her'. Claverhouse argued that Jean, being 'right principled', would not have married him if she had thought he was '. . . a persicutor, as they call me'.

Lady Dundee saw very little of her husband during the five years of their marriage, for his campaigns kept him away from Dudhope for long stretches. If Dundee's allegiance to the king did not supersede his allegiance to his wife, it certainly equalled it, and even on his wedding day he was called away to hunt out a conventicle (a secret prayer meeting). He was furious at being denied his wedding feast and wrote: 'I shall be revenged some time or other of this unseasonable trouble these dogs give me. They might have let Tuesday pass'.

Dundee's only son died in December 1689, five months after Killiecrankie, and Jean Cochrane and her son by her second husband were killed at an inn at Utrecht, Holland when the roof fell in.

13. THE PIPER O' DUNDEE

From Hogg's *Jacobite Relics of Scotland* (1819-21). The tune has been called 'The Drummer', 'The Tailor', 'For Weel he Kenned the Way O', and 'Good Morrow to your Night Cap'.

'The Piper o' Dundee' is a Jacobite song full of obscure references, and there is some confusion as to its origin and meaning. As early as the fifteenth century most towns in Scotland employed a town piper and drummer as servants of the burgh. The piper's duties were to play through the streets in the morning to waken people for work, and to play at the inspection of the marches and at elections and other official ceremonies. There are records of the Dundee town piper's duties starting at 4 a.m. and of his being paid 12d every year by every householder in the town.

The Rev. W. C. Skinner, in his book *The Barronie of Hilltowne, Dundee* (1927), claims that the 'Piper o' Dundee' was a man called Anthonie Court, a town piper who reputedly betrayed his loyalty to the town by playing the slogan tune of a rival party. The town piper had his duties clearly defined, and was supposed to be neutral in political matters; Court was censured and a proclamation was made that '. . . Anthonie Court, the common piper, having playit some springs throw the Burgh to the miscontent of honest neighbours, irritating and provoking some of the inhabitants to grite anger . . . likely to breid griter sedition . . . was ordainit not to play that spring called 'Tobacco, or The Laird Tin the Gauntlet', under quhatsoever uther name, either privily in men's houses, or publicly on the streets, at any time under pain of banishment'.

Although this was a genuine event, it is unlikely that it was the subject of the song 'The Piper o' Dundee'. It is possible that the song, in the form that we know it, was based on an older song which has been lost, but it is plain that the references in the song are not about local politics but the wider issue of the Jacobites.

Amulree in Perthshire was a place of secret meetings amongst partisans of the Stuart cause, and is the setting for the song. All the men mentioned were Jacobite leaders, some of whom had fought at the Battle of Sheriffmuir in 1715. The battle was fought between the Earl of Mar's troops, in favour of the Stuarts, and the Duke of Argyll's royalist army. There is some doubt as to who actually won the battle, as the old ballad suggests: 'There's some say that we wan, some say that they wan'. Many of the participants fled the field, and in 'The Battle of Sherramoor' by Burns, the men of Dundee and Angus appear to have been the fastest runners:

My sister Kate cam' up the gate
Wi' crowdie unto me, man;
She swoor she saw some rebels run
To Perth and to Dundee, man;
Their left-hand general had nae skill;
The Angus lads had nae gude will,
That day their neebour's blude to spill;
For fear by foes that they should lose
Their cogs o' brose, they scar'd at blows
And hameward fast did flee, man.

The song 'The Piper o' Dundee' suggests that 'brave Carnegie' of Findhaven is the hero of the song, but he also has the reputation of having been the 'best flier from the field of Shirramuir'. The old book *The Bards of Angus and the Mearns* claims that rather than Carnegie it was James, Earl of Southesk, named as the 'brave, generous Southesk' in the Sheriffmuir ballad, who was the Piper o' Dundee.

Whoever the renowned Piper o' Dundee was, what we have left is a fine song from the Jacobite era.

In the second verse, 'Auld Stuart's back again' might refer to James III, the 'Old Pretender', who returned to Scotland for the 1715 uprising.

14. THE TAY BRIDGE DISASTER

From the singing of Mrs Balfour of Lindores, Fife. Collected by Peter Shepheard.

'TERRIBLE ACCIDENT ON BRIDGE — ONE OR MORE OF HIGH GIRDERS BLOWN DOWN. AM NOT SURE AS TO THE SAFETY OF LAST TRAIN FROM EDINB- WILL ADVISE FURTHER ——'. So read the telegram from Dundee to railway staff in Edinburgh on the night of December 28th, 1879. While the disaster was not the worst railway accident in Scotland (in terms of number of deaths), it is certainly the best remembered and perhaps the most horrific.

The bridge had been hailed as a marvellous feat of engineering. At the time it was the longest bridge of its type in the world, and dignitaries from all over the world came to see it under construction. Among them were the Emperor of Brazil, Prince Leopold of Belgium and General Ulysses Grant, ex-President of the U.S.A. It was the fulfilment of a dream for designer Thomas Bouch, but later there were accusations of the use of 'Beaumont Egg' – a mixture of beeswax and iron filings often used cosmetically to conceal holes in defective iron castings. That night in December 1879 the central girders of the bridge were blown down by the ferocious winds which were sweeping all Scotland. The Edinburgh train left Burntisland at 5.27 and passed through Wormit just after 7 p.m. The seventy-five passengers on board the train all perished, and twenty-nine bodies were never recovered. In an inquiry into the disaster, it was found that the design, construction and maintenance were all at fault and Bouch, who had also planned to bridge the Forth, was blamed for the incident. His health deteriorated and he died a few months later.

This ballad was also printed by the Poets' Box, but Mrs Balfour's version has two extra verses, showing that the traditional currency of the song is not only dependent on the Poets' Box sheet.

While other ports in the British Isles, like Liverpool, Hull and Southampton, have to some extent retained their importance, Dundee is hardly known now for its involvement with sea traffic. The importance of the sea to Dundee's prosperity and day-to-day life is very little compared to a century ago, yet at one time Dundee's harbour was an exciting place, bustling with ships and sailors from all over the world. A nineteenth-century Canadian shanty had as one of its verses:

> Were you ever in Dundee,
> Bonnie laddie, Highland laddie,
> There some pretty ships you'll see,
> My bonnie Highland laddie.

By the 1870s a stretch of a mile or two from Craig Pier to Camperdown Dock was occupied by shipbuilding and timber yards, and the port employed five or six thousand men and boys. The growth and development of the town relied as much on the extent and efficiency of the harbour as the harbour relied on the prosperity of the town, so that each new breakthrough was a benefit to both.

The situation of Dundee has the special advantage of being beside a sheltered reach of a navigable river, the Tay estuary. It was probably the ease with which Dundee could trade with Dutch, French, Danish and Swedish ports that gave the town its beginnings. The Forth and the

7. Dock Street.

exposed harbours of Fife were dangerous going in stormy weather, so from the early days sailing ships would make for the calm of the Tay. The harbour at Dundee was known to be of some importance in the eleventh century, and in 1651, when General Monck captured Dundee during the Cromwellian civil wars, there were a hundred ships at the port.

The damage caused by Monck was significant, and it was not until the eighteenth century, when trade increased after the Union of Parliaments, that Dundee's harbour was extensively repaired.

The nineteenth century, with the changes brought by the industrial revolution and further increases in trade, saw Dundee's harbour and docks expand to a great extent. Jute had been trickling into the town during the 1830s, and in 1840 the barque *Selma* brought the first quantity of jute direct from Calcutta. There was a schooner leaving for London once a week and a steamer every fortnight; traders left for Leith three days a week and for Glasgow twice a week. With the whaling fleet, Crimean War supply ships (in the 1850s) and emigrant ships added to the harbour traffic, the tonnage increased from about 10,000 at the turn of the nineteenth century to almost 400,000 in 1866.

Music and song were a very important part of life aboard the large ships of the nineteenth century – the clippers, the jute cargo ships and the whalers – and to lighten the pulling jobs (hoisting sails, raising anchors and working the pumps) the sailors sang songs known as shanties or chanties. French Canadian lumberjacks sang a similar class of song while hauling logs, and it is generally thought that 'shanty' is a British corruption of the French word 'chanter' – to sing. There were different types of shanty to suit the various jobs on board. 'We're Bound to St. Peter's' was probably a *short-haul* shanty, sung during quick operations, while another type of shanty was a *halyard* shanty, used for jobs too heavy and prolonged for short-haul. These halyards were simple and regular in form, and each verse had four lines: a solo line, followed by one for the chorus, then a new solo line, and a final chorus. 'How Cauld These Winds' is a fragment of a much longer song which was possibly sung in a shanty setting, but like probably scores of Dundee songs of the sea, it has been lost to time.

The industry which probably brought more sea songs to Dundee from all over the world was whaling. It has long since gone from the town, but evidence of its existence remains in street names such as East Whale Lane, Baffin Street and Melville Street. Public houses with names such as 'The Arctic' and 'The Terra Nova' recall the great whaling ships of the nineteenth century. The *Arctic* was a whaler which was twice crushed into the ice in the Greenland sea – the second time it did not survive. The *Terra Nova* was another Arctic ship but was later used by Scott in his expedition to the South Pole.

Dundee's involvement with whaling lasted for about 150 years until the

8. Dundee fishing fleet leaving harbour.

start of World War One, and at one point it was the whaling capital of Britain. Other ports suffered because of the introduction of substitutes for whale oil, which was then used in street lighting, and because of over-efficiency in whale hunting, causing a scarcity of whales in the Arctic Sea. Dundee continued to send ships north long after Hull, the last English whaling port, ceased in 1866. The expanding jute trade used whale oil to soften the rough jute fibre, so with a ready market at home the Dundee whaling fleet flourished for years after the others failed.

With the improved railway services and the Tay bridges, and the demise of the whaling and jute industries, there is not much need now for the extensive dockland Dundee built in the nineteenth century. Much of the harbour has been reclaimed for the approach roads to the Tay road bridge, some new building ventures and the Swimming Pool and Leisure Centre. Although there is still the occasional sight of groups of visiting seamen from foreign navies wandering the city centre, these are unusual events for a town which once derived much of its livelihood from the sea. The few remaining Dundee sailing songs give a glimpse of that time and serve as a testament to a bygone age.

15. THE LANG AWA SHIP

1. On a bonnie green knowe, by the side of the sea, Sat a sailor's wife and

her bairnies three; And they sang as the wee waves gaed and cam',

'It's braw to sit and see the ships comin' in.'

CHORUS: Oh it's braw to sit and see the ships comin' in, Oh it's braw to sit and

see the ships comin in, They sang as the wee waves gaed and cam',

It's braw to sit and see the ships comin' in.

2. Oh, an outward bound may be fair to see,
   Wi the white sails set to the breezes free;
   But to gladden the heart I'm sure there's nane
   Like the sicht o' a lang awa ship comin hame.

3. A wee boat has left the big ship's side,
   It skims ower the tap o' the glancin' tide,
   The keel's on the beach, and the sailor free;
   He's hame to his wife and his bairnies three.

4. To a canty ingle and a clean hearth stane,
   They welcome the sailor to his hame again,
   And wi gratefu' hearts they praise His name,
   Wha's Power gar'd the lang awa ship come hame.

39

16. THE SAILOR LADDIE I

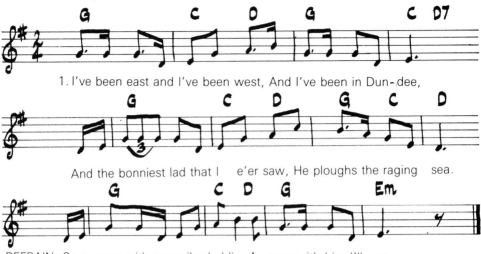

1. I've been east and I've been west, And I've been in Dun-dee,

And the bonniest lad that I e'er saw, He ploughs the raging sea.

REFRAIN: So a-way with my sailor laddie, A-way with him I'll go.

2. I've been east and I've been west,
   And I've been in Montrose,
   And the bonniest lad that e'er I saw,
   He wears the tarry clothes.

17. THE SAILOR LADDIE II

1. He skips upon the plainsteens,
   He sails upon the sea
   He's a bonny sailor laddie
   The lad that I gang wi.

2. His jersey's o' the bonnie blue,
   His troosers are o' white,
   He's a curly kep wi a tinsel band,
   The sailor's my delight.

3. I saw ma laddie gang awa,
   I saw ma lad set sail,
   I saw him turn his ship aboot,
   Awa to catch a whale.

4. He bade me aye keep up ma hert,
   He bade me nae be dull,
   He bade me aye keep up ma hert,
   An' he'd tak me tull himsel'.

Collected by Maurice Fleming.

9. Dundee Harbour workers. In the background, a corner of the Victoria Arch, since demolished.

18. WE'RE BOUND TO ST PETER'S

1. We're bound to St Peter's for baccy and rum,
   Goodbye, fare ye well! Goodbye, fare ye well!
   We're bound to St Peter's for baccy and rum,
   Hurrah, my bully b'ys, homeward bound!

2. 'Tis home we are bound and 'tis home we must go,
   Goodbye, fare ye well! Goodbye, fare ye well!
   'Tis home we are bound and we cannot say No –
   Hurrah, my bully b'ys, eastward bound!
   Hurrah, my bully b'ys, Dundee bound!

Collected by Maurice Fleming.

19. FOONDRY LANE

1. There's a Juter and a Battener Sailing up the Tay, And a' the wives in Foondry Lane Are singing blithe the day. There'll be pennies for the bairnies, A pint for Jock and Tam, Money for the picters, The auld fowk get a dram.

2. We'll gie the secks the go by, We canna sew and eat, And fivepence for twenty-five Will no buy muckle meat. We'll hae steak and ingins frying, Lift oor claes a' oot the pawn, We'll gaither wulks and boil them In a corn beef can.

Words by Mary Brooksbank.
As sung by Mary Brooksbank.
Collected by Maurice Fleming.

42

20. OLD DUNDEE TOWN ONCE MORE

1. Oh, fare ye well my own dear love, Ten thousand times a-dieu,
For I am going to leave you now, Once more to part from you.
Once more to part from you, dear girl, You're the one that I a-dore,
But still I'll live in hopes to see Old Dundee town once more.
But still I'll live in hopes to see Old Dundee town once more.

2. When I am on the salt sea sailing,
   And you are far behind,
   Kind letters I will write to you
   Telling secrets of my mind.
   The secrets of my mind, dear girl,
   You're the one that I adore,
   But still I live in hopes to see
   Old Dundee town once more.

3. There's a storm coming o'er us,
   I know it is coming;
   The night is dark and stormy,
   We can scarcely see the moon.
   Our good old ship is tossed about,
   For the angry waters roar,
   But still I live in hopes to see
   Old Dundee town once more.

4. But now the storm is over,
   And we are safe on shore,
   We'll drink good health to all dear girls,
   And the one that I adore.
   We'll drink strong ale and brandy,
   We'll make the tavern roar,
   And when our money is all spent
   We'll go to sea once more.

21. DUNDEE ONCE MORE

1. In Dundee once more, It's the place that I a - dore, When we're in
Lochee we're aye longin' tae be, Back in Dun - dee once more.

2. In the berryfields once more,
   In the berryfields once more,
   When we're in Blairgowrie we're aye longin' tae be,
   Back in Dundee once more.

3. On the whalers once more,
   On the whalers once more,
   When we're in the Baltic Sea we're aye longin' tae be,
   Back in Dundee once more.

As sung by Mary Brooksbank.
Collected by Maurice Fleming.

44

22. FROM SWEET DUNDEE

1. From sweet Dundee where we set sail All with a sweet and a pleasant gale, With our ring-tails set all abaft our mizzen peak, For to see my jolly tars how she's scudding o'er the deep, REFRAIN: To my he – ri – ro, to my he – ri – ro, To my he – ri – ro rite fal de ral de day.

2. Now by and by there came a squall,
   Haul down your ring tails, our captain loudly bawls,
   Clew up your gallant top sails and take them in,
   Let two hands lay forward and your jib run down.

3. It's now our captain he goes down below,
   And he calls for his cabin boy little Joe,
   Saying: 'Bring me one stiff glass of grog,
   For it is far better weather down here below.'

4. Then our chief mate he goes down below,
   And he sups his grog just like so,
   And he never cries for Jack or Joe,
   He does all the bullying, and he goes down below.

23. THE DUNDEE WHALER

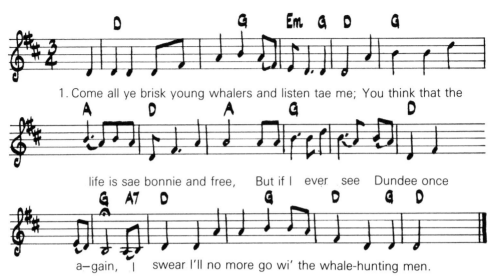

1. Come all ye brisk young whalers and listen tae me; You think that the life is sae bonnie and free, But if I ever see Dundee once a—gain, I swear I'll no more go wi' the whale-hunting men.

2. When the anchor is weighed and ye sail frae Dundee,
   The talk turns frae sweethearts tae the cauld Greenland sea,
   And if I ever see Dundee once again,
   I swear I'll no more go wi the whale-hunting men.

3. Ye'll get intae Lerwick tae fill up the stores,
   And ye'll spend a' your money on whisky and whores,
   But if I ever see Dundee once again,
   I swear I'll no more go wi the whale-hunting men.

4. With the sun and plain sailing ye think it's the game,
   Wi' the fog and the ice your thoughts turn tae hame,
   And if I ever see Dundee once again,
   I swear I'll no more go wi the whale-hunting men.

5. I've seen the auld whalers, they've lost their guid cheer,
   But they go back tae Newfoundland it's year efter year,
   But if I ever see Dundee once again,
   I swear I'll no more go wi the whale-hunting men.

Written by N. Gatherer.

24. HOW CAULD THOSE WINDS

How cauld those winds dae blaw, dear Lord!
What heavy draps o' rain!
I never had but ane dear love,
An' she is frae me ta'en.

Collected by Maurice Fleming.

46

25. THE *BALAENA*

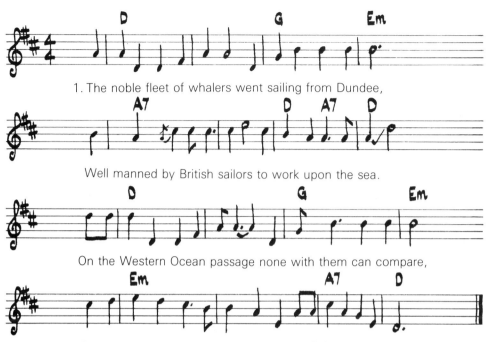

1. The noble fleet of whalers went sailing from Dundee,

Well manned by British sailors to work upon the sea.

On the Western Ocean passage none with them can compare,

But the smartest ship to make the trip is *Balaena* I declare.

Chorus:
For the wind is on the quarter and the engine's workin free,
There's no another whaler a-sailin fae Dundee,
Can beat the auld Balaena, so ye needn't try her on,
For we'll challenge a' baith large an' sma fae Dundee tae St John.

2. There's the new-built Terra Nova, a model with no doubt,
The Arctic and Aurora ye've heard so much about,
An' Jackman's model mailboat, the terror of the seas,
Couldn't beat the auld Balaena on a passage fae Dundee.

3. Now it happened on a Thursday, four days we'd left Dundee,
An' the wind blew on the quarter deck just aff the main ye see,
An' carried away oor bulwark, oor stanchions an' oor rails,
An' we left the whole concern, ma boys, a-floatin in the gales.

4. Bold Jackman carries canvas an' fairly raises steam,
An' Captain Guy in the Arran Boat goes ploughing through the stream;
An' Mullen declares the Eskimo would beat the bloomin lot,
But to beat the auld Balaena boys he'd find it rather hot.

47

10. The Dundee whaling ship *Balaena*.

5. And now that we are landed where the rum is very cheap,
   We'll drink success to the captain for ploughing us o'er the deep;
   A health tae a' oor sweethearts and tae oor wives sae dear,
   Not another ship could make the trip but the Balaena I declare.

As sung by Stewart Brown.

26. THE OLD *POLINA*

Sung to the tune of 'The *Balaena*' (No. 25)

Chorus:
Ooooh! The wind was on her quarter,
and the engines working free;
There's not another whaler
That sails the Arctic Sea
Can beat the Old 'Polina',
You needn't try; my sons,
For we challenged all, both great and small,
From Dundee to Saint John's.

1. There's a noble fleet of whalers, a-sailing from Dundee,
   Manned by Scottish sailors, to take 'em o'er the sea,
   On a western ocean passage, we started on the trip,
   And we flew along just like a song, on our gallant whaling ship.

2. 'Twas the second Sunday morning just after leaving port
   We met a heavy sou'west gale that washed away our boat;
   It swept away our quarterdeck, our stanchions went as well,
   An' the whole she-bang went floating in the waves and in the gale.

3. Art Jackson set his canvas, Fairweather got up steam,
   And Captain Guy, the daring b'y, came plunging through the stream;
   And Mullins in the 'Husky' tried to beat the bloody lot,
   But to beat the old 'Polina' was something he could not.

4. There's the noble 'Terra Nova', a model without a doubt,
   The 'Arctic' and 'Aurora' they talk so much about,
   Art Jackman's flying mail-boat, the terror of the sea,
   Tried to beat the old 'Polina' on a passage from Dundee.

5. We're back again in old St John's where rum and beer are cheap,
   An' we'll drink a health to Captain Guy who brought us o'er the deep;
   A health to all the girls out here and to our wives so fair,
   No other ship could make the trip with 'Polina' I declare.

Collected by Maurice Fleming.

27. BONNIE LADDIE, HIELAND LADDIE

1. "Whaur hae ye been a' the day, Bonnie Laddie, hieland laddie;

Whaur hae ye been sae lang away, My bonnie hieland laddie?"

"Well I've been takin fortune's road, Bonnie lassie, hieland lassie,

There's many at the whaling so I've been told, Ma bonnie hieland lassie."

2. 'I've shipped for the north on a Dundee whaler,
    Bonnie lassie, hieland lassie;
  Shipped for the North as a whaling sailor,
    Ma bonnie hieland lassie.'
  'But Greenland's shores are grey and cold,
    Bonnie laddie, hieland laddie,
  There's plenty ice but not much gold,
    Ma bonnie hieland laddie.'

3. 'When will you come back again,
    Bonnie laddie, hieland laddie;
  You an' a' the whalin men,
    Ma bonnie hieland laddie?'
  'Oh, I'll be back when I get hame,
    Bonnie lassie, hieland lassie,
  I'll gie up this whaling game,
    Ma bonnie hieland lassie.'

As sung by Jim Reid, Dundee.
Arranged by Peter Shepheard.

15. THE LANG AWA SHIP

Written by Isabella Boyd (1808-88) of Dundee, who was married to a tea and coffee merchant who would know all about sea trading.

Isabella Boyd wrote numerous poems and songs, and composed music for much of the latter, which were published by Methven and Simpson, although 'The Lang Awa Ship' was written to the tune 'O'er the Hills and Far Away'.

16. THE SAILOR LADDIE I

Collected by the Aberdeenshire folksong collector Gavin Greig (1856-1914) from the Rev. John Calder. In his notebooks it is known as 'Dundee', and it is related to a family of folksongs which include 'The Ploughboy Laddie', 'The Collier Laddie' and 'The Gypsy Laddies'. The tune is somewhat reminiscent of 'A Man's a Man for A' That'.

17. THE SAILOR LADDIE II

Collected by Maurice Fleming. The singer claimed that this song originated in Dundee.

18. WE'RE BOUND TO ST. PETER'S

Collected by Maurice Fleming, who writes: '*St Peter's* must be the French-owned island of Saint Pierre, near Miquelon. It cannot possibly be the little place in the South of Prince Edward Island, which is hardly worth a visit, where "baccy and rum" were no cheaper than in St John's, and which, in any case, lies off the course of boats homeward bound to Dundee from Newfoundland'. This song is quite evidently a shanty, although it is used as a song to accompany dancing in Newfoundland, when the band are resting in the bar.

19. FOONDRY LANE

Written by Mary Brooksbank, recorded by Maurice Fleming.

This song about the way individual prosperity was dependent on the incoming jute cargoes and ships is sung to the familiar 'Ball of Kirriemuir' tune.

Mary Brooksbank, on her first home when she was married in 1924 – a garret in Foundry Lane – said, 'when I first saw it I wept'.

20. OLD DUNDEE TOWN ONCE MORE

From a Poets' Box sheet.

This is a variant of a song which was chiefly known to sailors around the Bristol Channel area. The Welsh version (Old Swansea Town Once More) and the Irish one (The Holy Ground) are the most common. However there is one other Scottish variant called 'Campbeltown Once More'.

21. DUNDEE ONCE MORE

Written by Mary Brooksbank, recorded by Maurice Fleming.

This is obviously based on the previous song. Mary often based her songs on half-remembered fragments and snatches of traditional songs – the first verse of 'The Jute Mill Song' (No. 38) is based on a traditional rhyme. Dundee children still sing a verse similar to the second verse while on their way to the berryfields during the school holidays, and Amy Stewart Fraser has in her book *Dae Ye Min' Langsyne?* the following verse:

> Back in Edinburry once more,
> That's the toon that I adore,
> And I hope tae see,
> And I hope tae be
> In auld Edinburry once more.

22. FROM SWEET DUNDEE

Collected by George Gardiner and J. F. Guyer in 1906 from Frederick White of Southampton.

This is a bouncing version of a song generally known as 'Boston Harbour', said to have been very popular in the 1860s and '70s. The bold chorus is a feature of many sailing songs which are sung by the company.

23. THE DUNDEE WHALER

Written by Nigel Gatherer.

Life aboard the whaling ships was extremely rough. In 1829, ninety-two British ships were caught by pack ice in Baffin Bay, and in an incident known as the 'Baffin Bay Fair', men set free from some of the splintered ships wandered the ice drinking, rioting and looting. In 1837 the Dundee whaler *Arctic* returned to the town with seven of her original crew of forty-nine alive. Many whaler ships were lost and scurvy was very common.

It was customary in the nineteenth century for Dundee whaling ships to call in at Lerwick, Shetland to recruit more men. Shetlanders were regarded as more reliable than Dundee men, who would often go on shore for terrible drinking sprees.

24. HOW CAULD THOSE WINDS

Collected by Maurice Fleming, who writes, 'The very old man from whom I heard it told me that this was only the chorus of a very long song which the Dundee whalers brought over, and which, according to my old friend, "Dey'd be singin' dat sahng fur lahng toimes, aall de way tru".'

52

25. THE *BALAENA*

From the singing of Stewart Brown, singer with the Dundee folk group The Lowland Folk. He learned the song from the well-known Dorsetshire singer Cyril Tawney in the 1960s at the Dundee Folk Club in Roseangle. Cyril himself learned it from a singer in Lerwick, Shetland, and in *The Scottish Folksinger,* by Norman Buchan and Peter Hall, their version of *The Balaena* is from Bruce Laurenson of Lerwick.

The history of this song is a rather confusing one. On the one hand, it would seem to have been originally composed about another Dundee whaling vessel, the *Polynia,* as it mentions Captain Guy, who commanded the *Polynia* from 1883 until it was lost in 1891. However, according to the records of the *Balaena,* in 1904 the ship came back from the Davis Straits with one whale, four bears, ten tons of oil and 15cwt of bone, having been commanded by a Captain Guy. Whichever ship was the original subject of the song, we are left with many fine versions.

The *Balaena,* a Norwegian-built auxiliary steam whaler introduced into the Dundee fleet in 1891, was one of the last ships in the fleet to sail from the town. At the outbreak of the war in 1914, the *Balaena* was attached to the Hudson Bay Company, to supply munitions to Russia, but, badly overloaded, she sank during a gale in the White Sea on her first voyage.

26. THE OLD *POLINA*

Collected by Maurice Fleming.

'The Old Polina', also known as 'A Noble Fleet of Sealers', is how the Canadians refer to the song known in Britain as 'The *Balaena*'. The title is a Newfoundland mispronunciation of the name *Polynia,* which was a whaler and sealer from Dundee which spent the summer whaling in the North Atlantic and the winter plying the seal fishery off Newfoundland. Built in Dundee in 1861, the *Polynia* was a 472-ton vessel owned by the Dundee Seal and Whale Fishing Company. The skipper, Captain William Guy, commanded the ship from 1883 until it was crushed by ice in 1891, and, in the late 1890s, he became captain of the pleasure steamer running between Perth and Newburgh after retiring from deep-sea sailing.

All the other ships mentioned in the song are Dundee whalers, who would compete with each other to make the fastest trip on 'the Western Ocean passage' – one reason being that the first ship in St John's would have the pick of the experienced whale-hunting men.

The confusion about the original subject of the song has already been pointed out, but the probability lies with the *Polynia.* There are far more collected versions in Newfoundland and the rest of Canada than in Britain, and they all name the *'Polina'.* Also, in 1891 on the passage to Newfoundland, the *Polynia* was damaged in a gale, which is possibly the subject of the second verse.

27. BONNIE LADDIE, HIELAND LADDIE

This very fine whaling song was learned by Jim Reid from Archie Fisher. Recorded by Peter Shepheard.

'A Warning Tak By Me'

The popular bawdy ballad has always been with us. Songs pertaining to the sexual act stretch from the old ballads such as 'The Keech in the Creel' to the bothy ballads of the nineteenth century and the 'rugby songs' of the twentieth. While the Church in Scotland ranted against the sins of the flesh, the common people celebrated the act of love in song and verse. Burns, who loved this type of song, compiled a collection of bawdy ballads for private circulation among his friends. Many of the better songs Burns rewrote with more acceptable lyrics for Johnson's *Musical Museum* (1839).

The Church was particularly engaged in trying to curb the sexual activities of unmarried couples. One sanction in the seventeenth century was the 'stool of repentance', on which illicit fornicators were made to sit in shame in front of the congregation until penance was done. Despite the efforts of the Church, illegitimacy was rife in nineteenth-century Scotland. Aberdeenshire was particularly notorious, with almost one child in five being born illegitimate at one point. The illegitimacy ratio in Dundee itself, between 1861-1889, rose from about 8% to over 10%, while the figures for Scotland in general were falling.

Apart from the rising population in Dundee at the time, there are other possible reasons for this reversal of the trend. Country girls coming into a large, industrial town for work would be understandably disorientated, and might look for a lover for some sense of stability. In traditional rural society, where sex between couples was understood to lead to marriage, property and family ties provided pressure to make sure that this happened, but in the city there were no such pressures. A result of this was many frustrated courtships and many abandoned, pregnant women. Some women may have become pregnant in order to bring about a marriage, but without the weight of the community behind them this could not be enforced.

The theme of the abandoned pregnant woman is a popular one in folksong, and it is told from both points of view. Tales of the 'roving lads' who 'please the fair' and escape to love again, like 'Jockey's Escape from Dundee' and 'The Cooper o' Dundee', are found all over the British Isles. The practice of running away from a pregnant lover was common, the guilty party usually enlisting in the army or emigrating. 'The Braw Servant Lass' tells of a servant maid who went to every social occasion and 'at each new meetin' she'll get a new love':

> When some o' her sweethearts ken something is wrang,
> Into the same country they'll no' tarry lang,
> But rin aff to America, oh! sic a trick!
> And missie, poor thing, gets the whip staff to lick.

The other side of the story is well represented in folksong too – the broken-hearted girl lamenting the sad mistakes of her innocence. Victorian broadside ballads and songs abound with stories warning young girls to beware of loose company.

Another type of folksong which was very popular was the warning stories to men – tales of men being outwitted and robbed by 'young charmers' of 'watch-chain and purse', and often dignity as well. These misadventures often occurred to country folk coming into the town, and sometimes had a moralistic element. The most famous of this type of song from Dundee is a series of songs all centred around the Overgate, one of the oldest, most colourful, and, at one time, most notorious streets in the town.

The Overgate ran for a quarter of a mile from the north-west corner of the High Street up to the West Port. It was a collection of different and contrasting styles of architecture: a pot pourri of tenements, houses, shops and wynds which had a peculiar character of its own. In the 1883 *Ordnance Gazetteer of Scotland* it was said that the Overgate 'exhibits . . . an utter recklessness of architectural taste or uniformity'.

From its early days, many aristocrats had their town mansions in the Overgate (then called the Argyllgate, after the Marquis of Argyll). Over the years, however, it became less and less respectable, until by the late nineteenth century it was a rather run down and squalid affair, housing prostitutes, beggars and the like.

It was during the fairs that the Overgate was at its busiest. Ploughmen, bothy chiels and farmers from miles around would come into the town to arrange 'fees' (engagements for work on the farms). The fees were discussed over a pint of ale or two, and the Overgate, with its plentiful public houses, was the ideal place. Once the fees were secured, the bothy men were ready to celebrate. The shops, cheap restaurants, buster stalls, pubs and itinerant musicians made the Overgate the centre of activity.

There was an old saying – 'Fife for horses, the Mearns for women, and Dundee for a coggie o' guid ale!' Of course, the Overgate in Dundee was the place to go to for women, being notorious for its 'lowffs' (brothels). As the Perthshire singer Belle Stewart says, 'Ye could get anything in the Overgate, especially a nice young lady; they were specially obligin'.'

11. The Overgate in the late nineteenth century. Some children go barefoot.

28. JOCKEY'S ESCAPE FROM DUNDEE

Sung to the tune of 'Scots Callan o' Bonnie Dundee (No. 58)

1. Where got thou the haver-meal bannock?
   Blind Bubby, canst thou not see?
   I got them out of a Scotch man's wallet,
   As he lay easing under a tree.
   > Come fill up my cup, come fill up my can,
   > Come saddle my horse and call up my man,
   > Come open the gates and let me go free,
   > And shew me the way from bonny Dundee.

2. For I have neither rob'd nor stolen,
   Nor have I done any injury,
   But I have got a fair maid with bairn,
   The minister's daughter of bonny Dundee.
   > Come fill up my cup, come fill up my can,
   > Come saddle my horse and call up my man,
   > Come open the gates and let me go free,
   > For I'se gang no more to bonny Dundee.

3. Although I've gotten her maidenhead,
   Good sooth I've given her mine in lieu,
   For when at her daddie's I'se gang to bed,
   I'se kiss her without any more ado.
   > I's cuddle her close, and give her a kiss,
   > Pray tell me now where is the harm in this?
   > Then open the gates and let me go free –
   > For I'se gang no more to bonny Dundee.

4. All Scotland ne'er had such a lass,
   So bonny and blythe, as Jenny my dear,
   I given her a gown of green on the grass,
   But now I no longer must tarry here.
   > Then saddle my nagg that's bonny and gay,
   > For now it is time to go hence away,
   > Then open the gates and let me go free,
   > She's ken me no more in bonny Dundee.

5. In liberty still I reckon to reign,
   For why I have done no honest man wrong,
   The Parson may take his daughter again,
   For she'll be a mammy before it's too long.
   > And have a young lad or lass of my breed,
   > For I have done her a general deed,
   > Then open the gates and let me go free,
   > For I'se gang no more to bonny Dundee.

6. Since Jenny the fair was willing and kind,
   And came to my arms with right good will;
   A token of love I've left her behind,
   Thus have I requited my kindness still.
   > Tho' Jenny the fair I often had kissed,
   > Another may reap the Harvest I sow'd,
   > Then open the gates and let me go free,
   > And I'll never come more to bonny Dundee.

7. Her dad would have me to make her my bride,
   But to have and to hold, I could never endure,
   From bonny Dundee this day I will ride,
   It being a place not safe and secure.
   > Then Jenny farewell, my joy and my dear,
   > With sword in my hand the passage I'll clear,
   > Then open the gates and let me go free,
   > For I'se gang no more to bonny Dundee.

8. My father he is a muckle good laird,
   My mother a lady bonny and gay,
   Then while I have strength to handle a sword,
   The parson's request I'll never obey.
   > Then Sandy my man, be thou of my mind,
   > In bonny Dundee we's never be confin'd,
   > The gates we will force to let ourselves free,
   > And never come more to bonny Dundee.

9. Then Sandy replied, I'll never refuse,
   To fight for a laird so valiant and bold,
   While I have a drop of blood for to loose,
   E'er any fickle loon shall keep me in hold.
   > With sword in my hand, I'll valiantly stand,
   > And fight by your side to kill or be kill'd,
   > For forcing the gates, and let ourselves free,
   > And so bid adieu to bonny Dundee.

10. With sword ready drawn they rode to the gate,
    Where being denied an entrance through,
    The master and man they fought at that rate,
    That some ran away, and others they flew.
    > Thus Jockey the laird and Sandy the man,
    > They valiantly fought as Highlanders can,
    > In sight of the loons they set themselves free,
    > And so bid adieu to bonny Dundee.

29. THE COOPER O' DUNDEE

Sung to the tune of 'Scots Callan o' Bonnie Dundee' (No. 58).

1. Ye coopers and hoopers attend to my ditty,
   I sing o' a cooper wha dwelt in Dundee;
   This young man he was baith am'rous and witty,
   He pleased the fair maids wi the blink o' his ee.
   He wasnae a cooper, a common tub hooper,
   The maist o' his trade lay in pleasin the fair;
   He hoopt them he coopt them, he bort them, he plugt them,
   An' a' sent for Sandy when oot o' repair.

2. For a twelve month or sae this youth was respected,
   An' he was as busy as weel he could be;
   But business increased so that some were neglected,
   Which ruined trade in the town o' Dundee,
   A baillie's fair daughter had wanted a coupin,
   And Sandy was sent for, as oft time was he;
   He yerked her sae hard that she sprung an end-hoopin,
   Which banished poor Sandy frae Bonnie Dundee.

30. THE DUNDEE WEAVER

1. Oh, I'm a Dundee weaver and I come frae bonnie Dundee, I met a Glesca feller and he came courtin' me; He took me oot a-walking doon by the Kelvin Ha', And there the dirty wee rascal stole my thingumyjig awa', And there the dirty wee rascal stole my thingumyjig a – wa'.

2. He took me oot a picnic doon by the Rookin Glen,
   He showed tae me a bonnie wee bird an' he showed me a bonnie wee hen;
   He showed tae me a bonnie wee bird fae a linnet tae a craw,
   He showed tae me the bird that stole ma thing-a-me-jig awa,
   He showed tae me the bird that stole ma thing-a-me-jig awa.

3. Now I'll gang back tae Dundee lookin' bonnie, young an' fair,
   And I'll pit on my bucklin' shoes an' tie up ma bonnie broon hair;
   And I'll pit on ma corsets tight tae mak ma body look sma,
   An' wha will ken wi' ma rosy cheeks ma thing-a-me-jig's awa,
   An' wha will ken wi' ma rosy cheeks ma thing-a-me-jig's awa.

4. Come a' ye Dundee weavers, tak this advice fae me,
   Never let a fellae an inch above yer knee;
   Oh never stand at the back o' the close or up against the wa',
   For if ye dae ye can safely say yer thing-a-me-jig's awa,
   For if ye dae ye can safely say yer thing-a-me-jig's awa.

As sung by Stewart Brown, Dundee.
Arranged by Peter Shepheard.

31. THE OVERGATE A

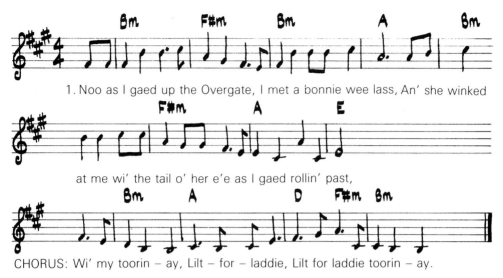

1. Noo as I gaed up the Overgate, I met a bonnie wee lass, An' she winked

at me wi' the tail o' her e'e as I gaed rollin' past,

CHORUS: Wi' my toorin – ay, Lilt – for – laddie, Lilt for laddie toorin – ay.

2. I asked her if she'd tak a gless,
   She said she'd like that fine,
   Says I, 'I'm ower frae Auchtermuchty
   Tae the market wi some swine.'

3. I took her tae a sittin room,
   A wee bit doon the burn,
   Aye it's true whit Rabbie Burns has said,
   A man was made tae mourn.

4. For o' hot pies and porter,
   She ate them by galore,
   She ate an' drank as much tae serve
   An elephant for a year.

5. Then we baith gaed up the stairs
   Tae hae a contentit nicht,
   When an a'fu knock cam tae the door
   At the breakin o' the licht.

6. It was a big fat boaby
   He gat me by the tap o' the hair,
   An' he gied me the whirlijig
   Richt doon tae the fit o' the stairs.

7. Noo I gaed up the stairs again,
   I wis seekin oot ma claes;
   Says the polisman, 'Get oot o' this
   Or I'll gie ye sixty days!'

8. Says I, 'I've lost my waistcoat,
   My watch-chain and my purse',
   Says she, 'I've lost my maidenheed
   An' that's a damn sight worse!'

9. Noo, I'll gae back tae Auchtermuchty,
   Contentit I will be,
   Wi the breakin o' ma five pound note
   Wi a lassie in Dundee.

As sung by Belle Stewart.
Collected by Maurice Fleming.

THE OVERGATE B

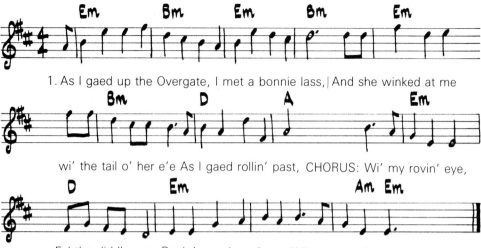

1. As I gaed up the Overgate, I met a bonnie lass, | And she winked at me

wi' the tail o' her e'e As I gaed rollin' past, CHORUS: Wi' my rovin' eye,

Fal the diddle eye, Rovin' eye dum derry, Wi' my rovin' eye.

2. 'What is your name my bonny lass,
   What is your name my lammie?'
   Right modestly she answered me:
   'My name is Bonny Annie.'

3. 'How old are you my bonny lass,
   How old are you my honey?'
   She answered me right saucilie:
   'I'm sixteen years come Sunday.'

4. 'If I should come tae your bower door,
   When the moon is shining clearly,
   It's will ye rise and let me in
   That your mammy widna hear ye?'

5. An' when I cam' tae her bower door,
   I found the lassie wauken;
   But lang before the grey morn cam'
   The auld wife heard us talkin'.

6. She gaed tae the fire tae blaw the coal,
   Tae see if she wid ken me,
   But I kicked the auld runt in the fire
   And bade my heels defend me.

7. Oh, fare thee weel, my bonnie lass,
   Oh, fare thee weel my lammie;
   Ye are a gay and a bonnie lass
   For a' your waukrife mammy.

As sung by Jim Reid.

63

32. THE BEEFCAN CLOSE

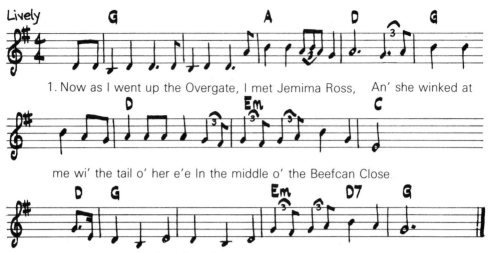

1. Now as I went up the Overgate, I met Jemima Ross, An' she winked at me wi' the tail o' her e'e In the middle o' the Beefcan Close.

CHORUS: Ricky doo dum day, Doo dum day, Ricky dicky doo dum day.

2. I asked her who she stayed with,
   An' she said it was Mistress Bruce,
   An' after that I got an in-
   vitation till her hoose.

3. When I went up the close that nicht,
   The stairs wis awfy dark,
   So I took ma money fae my inside pooch,
   An' I tied it tae the tail o' ma sark.

4. When I went in the hoose that nicht,
   I ower tae the chair sat doon,
   But she winked at me wi the tail o' her ee,
   An' she says, 'Come ben the room.'

5. Now a' that nicht I dreamt I wis in
   The airms o' Jemima Ross,
   But when I woke up I wis on ma back
   In the middle o' the Beefcan Close.

6. Now a' ye lads an' lassies here,
   When ye gang oot for a lark,
   Jist be like me when ye're on a spree
   Tie the money tae the tail o' yer sark.

7. An' now my song is ended here,
   I hope you enjoyed it well,
   An' when you go up the Overgate,
   See an' enjoy yersel'.

As sung by Annie Watkins.
Collected by Maurice Fleming, arranged by Peter Shepheard.

12. The Beefcan Close.

33. BEWARE OF AN ABERDONIAN A

1. I've had misfortunes ane an' twa, They're no worth while tae mention,
But I'll tell ye ane that bangs them a', Gin ye gie me at-tention.
Ae nicht I left hame in Lochee, Wi twa or three lads tae hae a spree,
An' I daundered doon intae Dundee Where I met an Aber — donian.

CHORUS: It's oh young men where e'er ye be, If ever ye gang on a spree,
I hope ye'll aye be advised by me Tae beware o' an Aberdonian.

2. That nicht when gaun doon Nethergate,
   I met that handsome charmer,
   She asked me for tae stand her a treat,
   O' something hot tae warm her.

   So intae a refreshment hoose we went,
   An' baith sat doon wi ae consent
   When soon ten shillings there I spent,
   Tae treat my Aberdonian.

   Chorus:

66

3. She ate two dozen o' tuppeny pies,
   She drank two quarts o' porter,
   For the bowls o' tripe she quickly cries,
   An' the tatties I had bought her.

   A board o' oysters tae that nicht,
   It very soon gaed oot o' sicht,
   An' I paid for a' they served me richt,
   Tae treat that Aberdonian.

   Chorus:

4. She put some stuff intae my drink,
   Which sent ma head a reeling,
   The hoose ran roond an' ma een did blink
   An' I lost baith sense an' feeling.

   For when I wakened up again,
   I missed ma purse ma watch an' chain,
   An' I never since saw them again,
   Nor yet my Aberdonian.

   Chorus:

5. She taen my new Balmoral cap,
   Ma shoon an' monkey jacket,
   I am the most unlucky chap,
   Sae awfae shy an' glaikit.

   It's ever since I'm nearly mad,
   If ever I chance tae meet that jaud,
   I'll surely send her tae the quad,
   The faithless Aberdonian.

   Chorus:

6. She teached a lesson untae me,
   As long as I am living,
   Oh never again tae mak sae free,
   Wi' lassies sae deceiving.

   If ever I think tae chance my life,
   An' tak untae masel a wife,
   I'd rather fa upon a knife,
   Than marry an Aberdonian.

   Chorus:
   There's nothing in this world that pleases me,
   Like a gey braw lass an a guid cup o tea,
   But ma mither aye said be advised by me,
   An beware o' an Aberdonian.

As sung by Eck Harley, Cupar.
Collected and arranged by Peter Shepheard.

BEWARE OF AN ABERDONIAN B

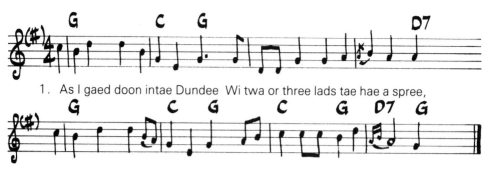

1. As I gaed doon intae Dundee Wi twa or three lads tae hae a spree,

I daundered doon intae Dundee, I met in wi' an Aber - donian.

2. For refreshments we a' went,
   We a' sat doon wi ae consent,
   Ten and sixpence there I spent,
   For tae treat my Aberdonian.

3. She eat two dozen o' tuppeny pies,
   Forbyes a glass o' porter,
   Wi the bowls o' tripe she pit oot o' sight,
   An' the tatties that I bought her.

4. I lost my purse an' ma watch an' chain,
   Never will I see them again,
   Never will I see them again,
   Nor yet my Aberdonian.

5. Nothing in the wide world pleases me,
   Like a fine wee lass an' a guid cup o' tea,
   Ma mother aye she said to me,
   To beware of an Aberdonian.

As sung by John White at Peat Inn, Fife.
Collected by Peter Shepheard.

68

34. THE BACK O RERES HILL A

1. Last year at Lady Mary's Fair when I wis in Dundee, I fell in wi' an auld sweetheart, an' he being on the spree, His company I did accept, and with him I did go, All to my sad misfortune, for it proved my overthrow.

2. We wandered East we wandered West we wandered roond the Law,
   He said he'd see me hame that nicht but hame I never saw,
   He kept beside me a' the time resolved tae hae his will,
   An' by an' by we lost our way at the Back o' Reres Hill.

3. So when we got tae Reres Hill the laddie says tae me,
   'We can't go home tonight ma dear it's far ower late you see,
   But the nicht is warm and in ma pooch I've got another gill,
   So let us lay doon here content at the Back o' Reres Hill.'

4. So syne we had a nip a-piece tae quieten oor alarms,
   When we awoke in the mornin we were locked in each other's arms,
   He handed me the bottle another glass tae fill,
   And I drank his health an' store o' wealth at the Back o' Reres Hill.

5. It's syne the laddie says tae me, 'Dear lassie dinna mourn,
   For while I draw the breath o' life frae you I'll never turn,
   And if ye'll come to yonder toon my wedded wife tae be,
   We'll be the happiest couple yet there is in a' Dundee.'

6. It's may I never prosper and may I never thrive,
   In anything I tak in hand as lang as I'm alive,
   If e'er I say I rue the day ma laddie had his will,
   Success tae Lady Mary's Fair an' the Back o' Reres Hill.

As sung by Eck Harley.
Collected and arranged by Peter Shepheard.

THE BACK O' RERES HILL B

Sung to the tune of previous song.

1. 'Twas on a Saturday evening when I went to Dundee,
   I fell in with an old sweetheart, and he being on the spree,
   In company we did agree, and with him I did go,
   And it's to my sad misfortune, it proved my overthrow.

2. I wandered east, I wandered west, his company to shun,
   Until the train it was away, nae mair for to return.
   My laddie followed after me, wi free and heart's guid will,
   It was that night I lost my way at the back o' Reres Hill.

3. When I awoke next morning, I was locked in my lover's arms,
   When I awoke next morning, from enjoying my lover's charms.
   My love gave me the bottle, another glass to fill,
   I drank his health, then we parted at the back o' Reres Hill.

4. Oh, my love wrote me a letter, which made me weep and mourn;
   He sent to me another that he would ne'er return.
   But if I'd come to sweet Dundee, his wedded wife to be,
   Wi' heart and hand in wedlock band, how happy we would be.

5. Oft in my lover's arms, my love to him I've told,
   And in my lover's arms he oft did me unfold;
   But girls, keep your secrets, let no one know your mind,
   That talks of love and marrying you, when it's far from his design.

6. Oh, may I never prosper, or may I never thrive,
   Nor anything I take in hand as long as I'm alive.
   And the very grass I walk on, may it refuse to grow,
   If I ever loved anyone as dear as I loved you.

7. So all ye Aberdeen lassies, a warning tak by me,
   And be sure and choose your company when ye gang intae Dundee,
   And beware of young bachelor laddies down by yon Baxter's Mill,
   For they're sure to gar ye lose your way at the back o' Reres Hill.

THE BACK O' RERES HILL C

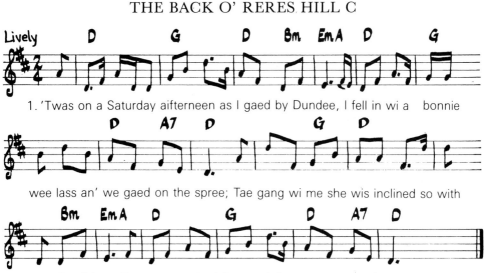

Lively

1. 'Twas on a Saturday aifterneen as I gaed by Dundee, I fell in wi a bonnie

wee lass an' we gaed on the spree; Tae gang wi me she wis inclined so with

me she did go, But to my sad misfortune it became my overthrow.

2. I'd been a single pooman lad until this very day,
   An' coorted every bonnie wee lass that ever came my way;
   But noo I'd met the bonniest yet, and firm it wis her will,
   She widna gang an' coort wi me tae the back o' Reres Hill.

3. Says I, 'The stars are shining bright,' says she, 'A wedding ring
   Shines twice as bricht, gie me its sicht, or ma love ye'll never win.'
   Says I, 'Ma lass drink up yer glass, if drink it up ye will,
   Sure a frew drams more and we'll be there at the back o' Reres Hill.

4. We drank till closin time wis by an' syne we drank the mair,
   Now whaur I thocht I had a wee lass I could swear I cam in wi a pair;
   Wi ma bleary eyes she looked so spry an' she wis sober still,
   And now says she, 'Come awa wi me tae the back o' Reres Hill.'

5. She marched along the Ferry Road an' up the Reres brae,
   I couldna get a sleep at a', for a sleep did I no pray,
   'But gin ye tak me for yer wife then sleep guid sir ye will,'
   I said, 'Aye, aye,' for I thocht I'd die at the back o' Reres Hill.

6. Now a' ye single poomen lads, a warning tak by me,
   Oh mind and choose yer company when ye gang intae Dundee.
   An' mind that awfie clever lass that works in the Halley's Mill,
   For she's a yae that'll hae her way at the back o' Reres Hill.

As sung by Stuartie Foy, Dundee.
Collected and arranged by Peter Shepheard.

35. THE MAGDALEN GREEN A

1. I am a brisk young sailor lad just newly come from sea;

My gallant ship lies anchored in the harbour o' Dundee.

Young Betsy being the fairest maid that e'er my eyes have seen,

I asked her wid she take a walk all along by the Magdalen Green.

2. A roguish smile upon her face, she answered me and said:
Kind Sir, I'd go along with you but you know I am afraid.
The paths they are so slippery, the night so cold and keen,
It would not do for me to fall down by the Magdalen Green.

3. With kind words and promises along with me she went,
We rambled here, we rambled there, on love and pleasure bent,
Day after day we met and roved about that pleasant scene,
I fear the maid had many a fall down by the Magdalen Green.

4. But soon the time for parting came, my ship had hoisted sail.
No longer could I see my dear, to tell love's pleasant tale.
We sang farewell to old Dundee, where I had happy been,
And she was left to walk alone down by the Magdalen Green.

5. As I lay in my berth one night when my weary watch was done,
I dreamt I was the father of a darling little son.
And in my dream his mother, too, right plainly she was seen,
And she was weeping bitterly down by the Magdalen Green.

6. Oh! When my ship puts in again at the harbour of Dundee,
I'll search the town all up and down until my girl I see.
I'll ask her to forgive me, for the rascal I have been,
And we will make it up again down by the Magdalen Green.

72

7. Come all ye jolly sailors bold, a warning take by me,
   And never slight a poor girl all for her poverty.
   To lightly love and sail away is neither straight nor clean,
   So never do as I once did down by the Madgalen Green.

As sung by Eck Harley.
Collected and arranged by Peter Shepheard.

THE MAGDALEN GREEN B

As sung by Jim Reid.
Arranged by Peter Shepheard.

36. DOWN BY THE YEAMAN SHORE

Sung to the tune of 'The Back o' Reres Hill' A (No. 34)

1. Come all ye swains of Scotland, I pray you lend an ear,
   And listen to this song of mine I'm going to let you hear,
   You've been to me an enemy, which grieves my heart full sore,
   And like a dart which pierced my heart down by the Yeaman Shore.

2. The first time that I saw my love it was into Dundee;
   It was on the streets of bonny Dundee, down by the banks of Tay;
   It was there I saw that fair maid, whom I've often seen before,
   So I'll have a walk, I love to talk down by the Yeaman Shore.

3. The next time I saw my love it was into spring,
   The trees they were a-budding, and the birds began to sing;
   I says, my pretty fair maid, would you take a walk once more,
   For I love to walk and talk with you down by the Yeaman Shore.

4. If I were to walk with you, I am afraid I would be seen,
   Or if I were to stay with you, they would wonder where I'd been;
   My parents they would angry be, and chide for evermore,
   If I were seen with anyone down by the Yeaman Shore.

5. If I had a fortune of twenty thousand pounds,
   I'd clothe with crimson and scarlet, with gold and silver round;
   I would give it all to my true love, though it were ten times more,
   For I love to walk and hear her talk down by the Yeaman Shore.

6. It's O if fortune would but prove this lassie to be mine,
   Or O if death would only come and take me out of pain;
   For she is daily on my mind, she's the girl whom I adore,
   For I love to walk and hear her talk down by the Yeaman Shore.

7. Come all ye swains of Scotland, I bid you all adieu;
   It's to some distant corner, I pray you take your flight;
   You may take them gently by the waist, as you've often done before,
   And give them a memorandum that they will mind, on the Yeaman Shore.

13. The Yeaman Shore.

28. JOCKEY'S ESCAPE FROM DUNDEE

From a broadside, 'To its own proper Tune'.

This broadside ballad has been mentioned in many collections since the eighteenth century, but printed in few because of its 'vulgarity'. Described as a 'remarkably coarse Grub St. song of licentious sentiment', it is sometimes ascribed to Thomas D'Urfey, as it appears in his *Pills to Purge Melancholy* (1719), but it was also a common broadside in the eighteenth century, so it is possibly earlier. The first verse is taken from the very old song 'Scots Callan of Bonny Dundee', and the tune given in *Pills* is a set of the ancient tune 'Adew Dundee' (see notes for 'Scots Callan' – No. 58). David Herd had the following verse in his *Ancient & Modern Scots Songs and Ballads* (1776):

> O have I burnt, or have I slain?
> Or have I done aught injury?
> I've gotten a bonny young lassie with bairn,
> The baillie's daughter of bonny Dundee.
> Bonny Dundee, and bonny Dundass,
> Where shall I see sae bonny a lass?
> Open your ports, and let me gang free,
> I maun stay nae longer in bonny Dundee.

29. THE COOPER O' DUNDEE

Collected by Robert Burns. The tune is 'Adew Dundee' (see notes for 'Scots Callan' – No. 58).

Ewan MacColl said of 'The Cooper of Dundee' that it is '. . . one of the many songs based on a theme which has been popular since the middle ages'. There is another song called 'Cuddy the Cooper' which was either written by Burns or merely collected by him, and which uses the same sexual imagery:

> There was a cooper they ca'd him Cuddy,
> He was the best cooper that I ever saw; .
> He came to girth our landladie's tubbie,
> He banged her buttocks agin the wa'.
>
> Cooper, quo' she, hae ye ony mony?
> The deevil a penny, quo' Cuddy, at a'!
> She took out her purse, an' she gied him a guinea,
> For banging her buttocks agin the wa'.

In Hogg's *Jacobite Relics of Scotland* (1819-21) there is a similarly named song, 'The Cooper o' Cuddy', which probably has the same tune, but which has quite different implications.

30. THE DUNDEE WEAVER

Recorded from Stewart Brown by Peter Shepheard.

This is a widely known song, but one which is not often sung because of its subject and nature. It is the sort of song which would be sung to folksong collectors only after the tape recorders had been switched off. Nevertheless, several versions have been recorded from both women and men. Matt McGinn wrote 'The Sequel to the Dundee Weaver' in 1968, taking the point of view of the 'Glesca Fellae' who has had a letter from the Dundee Weaver asking for money, claiming that he had 'put a canary in her cage':

> This wee Dundee weaver she must surely think me daft,
> I showed it to my cronies and they all stood there and laughed.
> They said that I should write to her and tell her tae get tae Hell,
> For everyone of them has had a canary there as well!

31. THE OVERGATE

A) From the singing of Belle Stewart, collected by Maurice Fleming. Also recorded by Belle on her L.P. 'Queen Among the Heather' on Topic 12TS307.

It would seem that there are no two similar versions of this song, and I have heard of arguments about which is the correct way to sing it. Of course, there is no *correct* way to sing it, but there are three distinctly different tales under the umbrella of 'The Overgate', and all of these tales get mixed up and elements of one will crop up alongside elements of another. Belle Stewart sings the first story, and all strains of it mention 'the burn', which is the Scourinburn, a street near the top of the Overgate near the West Port (now called Brook Street). David Cochrane, a singer from Coupar Angus, actually mentions the Scourinburn in his version, but most leave it as the more vague 'burn'. Belle usually adds a few verses near the end, all to do with life on the farm at Auchtermuchty where the lad is supposed to come from; for example:

> There is a maid upon the fairm,
> She is a dainty dame;
> She milks the kye at early morn,
> Gin dinner time it's cream.

B) From the singing of Jim Reid, who says, '. . . that song came to Dundee by way of a wandering minstrel from Freuchie called Singing Sandy, who used to change the name in the first line to suit the place he happened to be in at the time'. Burns collected a very similar song in Ayrshire called 'A Waukrife Minnie' for Johnson's *Musical Museum* (1787-1803). Both this version and the previous one are related to a large family of songs found throughout Britain and Ireland, other variants being called 'Wi My Rovin Eye', 'My Rolling Eye' and 'Seventeen Come Sunday'.

32. THE BEEFCAN CLOSE

Recorded from Annie Watkins by Maurice Fleming.

Jeannie Robertson sang a version of this song, but called it 'The *Buchan* Close': 'I asked her what her name might be, She said Jemima Ross, And I live in Blaeberry Lane, At the foot o' the Buchan Close'. It is of course another variation of 'The Overgate', but sung to the tune of 'The Keech in the Creel' with the famous 'Ricky doo dum day' chorus. Charles Lamb of Lochee had the following extra verse, which would appear to be missing from most other versions:

> Noo I gaed awa intae the room,
> Beside her I did creep;
> Me hain some beer, I felt gey queer,
> An I seen fell fast asleep.

The Beefcan Close was probably the local nickname of North George Street, off the Overgate, although Charlie Lamb's version has the location as 'Todburn Lane, At the back o' the Beefcan Close'.

33. BEWARE OF AN ABERDONIAN

A) Recorded from Eck Harley by Peter Shepheard.

Eck Harley based the words of his version on a sheet similar to the Poets' Box sheets, but printed in Edinburgh by C. Sanderson.

B) From the singing of John White at Peat Inn, Fife. Collected by Peter Shepheard.

This is an extremely clipped version of the song, having only four verses to the previous version's thirteen, but for all that it tells the story, getting rid of the 'dead wood' as so often happens in songs originating from printed sources. Elements of the song are reminiscent of 'The Overgate' A (No. 31), which possibly inspired it.

34. THE BACK O' RERES HILL

A) From the singing of Eck Harley, collected by Peter Shepheard.

Eck Harley uses the text on a Poets' Box sheet for his words of this song, but the Poets' Box also printed another quite different set of words (see next version). Although we know that Lady Mary Fair was held at Whitsun, there is some confusion as to where it was held. Some people say it was at the top of the Wellgate steps, while others maintain that it was held in the High Street and then moved to the Greenmarket. Reres Hill is in a park in Broughty Ferry.

B) Collated from a version in Ord's *Bothy Ballads* (1930) and a Poets' Box sheet.

The Poets' Box sheet gives the air as 'Down By the Yeaman Shore', and although there is no record of it, it is possible that Eck Harley's tune is in fact the missing air.

C) As sung by Stuartie Foy, Dundee, collected by Peter Shepheard.

Stuartie Foy is now ninety-two and has been married for seventy years. He says that that he learned these words as a boy and made up the tune. This is probably a mistake, as the tune is almost identical to a Scott Skinner quickstep called 'The Lovat Scouts', also claimed by Neil Grant in *Kerr's Andy Stewart Album* (1960), where Stewart has an extremely similar version to Stuartie Foy's.

35. THE MAGDALEN GREEN

A) From Eck Harley, recorded by Peter Shepheard. There are countless existing versions of this song, and while there is almost a different tune for each singer, the words are fairly standard. This may point to the Poets' Box sheet (from which Eck Harley got his words) being a common source. The last verse is not usually sung.

B) Jim Reid's tune, recorded by Peter Shepheard. Jim Reid says, 'Adam Young of Forfar . . . taught me *The Magdalen Green* about ten years ago. He himself got it more than forty years ago out of the Poet's Box'.

Magdalen in the song should be pronounced *Madlin* or *Medlin*. The Magdalen Green itself is a grassy slope near the north end of the Tay rail bridge. It probably got its name from the grounds belonging to the chapel dedicated to St Mary Magdalen. There is confusion as to who the land originally belonged to, but for hundreds of years it has been jealously claimed for the community of Dundee. Indeed, when the Laird of Blackness tried to reclaim his right of arable possession, the matter was referred to the Lords of Council and Session. They decreed that march stones should be placed along the boundary of the Green, and that all should heed the old warning to 'in na way transcend the auld marches of the Magdalen Gair'. The Magdalen Green figures throughout the history of Dundee as a place of public gathering and recreation. Whenever a threat to the town occurred, it was here that people congregated, 'weill coden in feir of weir' (well prepared for war), and in the 1840s the early Chartists met there to voice their demands.

36. DOWN BY THE YEAMAN SHORE

From a Poets' Box sheet.

No air is given, but on one of the 'Back o' Reres Hill' sheets the air is given as 'Down by the Yeaman Shore'. Eck Harley's, being the only tune found for 'Reres Hill', is possibly used for both songs.

The Yeaman Shore, a street at right angles to Union Street in the centre of Dundee, is now almost overshadowed by the complex of roads leading through the city and up to the road bridge. From the Yeaman Shore to the present railway station and the Esplanade is actually land reclaimed from the Tay in the nineteenth century for the building of the West Station (demolished in 1966) and some new railway lines.

The Mill, Marriage, and Unemployment

Dundee has been involved in many manufacturing industries, most of which flourished for a while and then failed. Names of streets were sometimes the only reminders of industries, examples being Bucklemaker's Wynd, Bonnet Hill, Butcher Row, Brewery Lane, Candle Lane and Cotton Road. Bonnet-making once employed a substantial proportion of the town's population, and for many years what is now called the Hilltown was called the Bonnet Hill, where the industry was centred. Victoria Road was originally called Bucklemaker's Wynd after the trade which thrived in that area. Seven different companies manufactured sewing thread, and seven different companies spun cotton. There were nine yards at which the tanning of leather was carried out. There was one industry, however, which persevered and developed into a greatly successful business – the jute industry.

There had been a linen spinning and weaving industry in Dundee for many years using imported flax from Russia, but the Crimean War halted imports, so it became necessary to find an alternative fibre which could be used on the same machinery. Earlier, in 1840, the first quantity of jute had been shipped direct from Calcutta, so jute was to some extent a tried and tested substitute, and in about 1856 most Dundee manufacturers switched to jute production.

From the latter half of the nineteenth century until the late 1960s, Dundee was the centre of a thriving jute industry, which employed a large segment of the town's labour, adults and children alike. For most of the twentieth century women dominated the workforce. Men were due pay rises at the ages of sixteen, eighteen and twenty-one, and employers often preferred to lay men off rather than grant the extra wages. There is some evidence to suggest that men were not keen to adopt the new power looms when they were introduced in the nineteenth century, and so the employers willingly replaced the workforce with women. This also ties in with the theory that the employers, keen to avoid strike action from the male unions, found women 'more manageable'. It was quite common for a married woman to go out to work at the mill, and for her husband to stay at home, looking after the house and children.

By 1930, about 17,000 people in the jute industry were out of work – this was about half the total workforce. At its worst the total was over 75 per cent, and the unemployment situation was highly serious. After 1935, with the threat of war looming on the horizon, the jobless total dropped sharply, with jobs to be found in the factories and foundries, and at the docks. For many years, however, the Great Depression meant poverty and humiliation for a large number of Dundee folk.

14. Jute mill workers.

Many people did not qualify for unemployment benefit, and there was a system of relief called 'transitional unemployment benefit', or 'the parish' as it was commonly known. To get this benefit impoverished men and women had to put their case to an officer at the Parish Council Office at Bell Street, near the centre of Dundee. The officer would decide there and then whether benefit would be paid, and sometimes personal hostility denied benefit to unfortunate applicants. The Clerk of Office at Bell Street was a particularly hard man called Robert Allan, known as Boaby Allan to the Dundonians, who generally detested him.

In 1931 the Means Test was introduced. A thorough examination of circumstances was ordered before parish relief could be paid, which meant that the officers had to visit people's houses and check coal bunkers, larders, etc., and the humiliation of such visits was felt by a large section of the community. Some officers were notorious for the lengths to which they would go to catch people out. Calls would be made early in the morning, before the household was up, or at any unexpected time.

A Glasgow street song of the time was about the Means Test Man:

> When ye hear me· rat-tat-tat upon the door,
> Have you money in the bank or money in the store?
> Ye'd better look oot or else ah'll get ye,
> For ah'm neither Santa Claus nor Doug-a-las-Fairbanks,
> I am the Means Test man!

Some officers would tell families to sell their properties, such as furniture, to raise money, thus denying them parish money on the Means Test. If a family could prove that their poverty was dire enough, they might be given a pound for essential food and coal.

Days of high unemployment are coming back to Dundee, but it is to be hoped that they will never be as bad as they were in the 1920s and '30s. The town is no longer dependent on just one main industry, and has diversified to an extent which should prevent the same mass unemployment. The improved social security system, although no substitute for a job, protects the unemployed from the humiliation of the Means Test. One can only hope for and look forward to a time when Dundee again has the prosperity she had before.

37. THE DUNDEE LASSIE

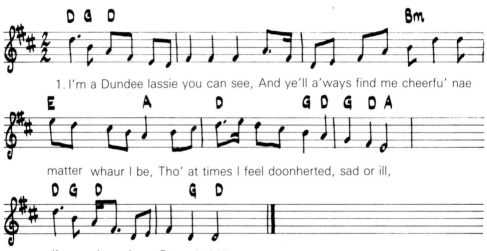

1. I'm a Dundee lassie you can see, And ye'll a'ways find me cheerfu' nae matter whaur I be, Tho' at times I feel doonherted, sad or ill, I'm a spinner intae Baxter's Mill.

2. My mither died when I was young, my faither fell in France,
I'd like tae hae been a teacher, but I never got the chance,
I'll soon be getting married tae a lad they ca' Tam Hill,
And he is an iler intae Halley's mill.

3. I'm chumming wi a lassie, they ca' her Jeannie Bain,
She says she'll never merry, her lad got killed in Spain,
I often hear her speak about a place they ca' Teruel,
And she is a winder intae Craigie's mill.

As sung by Mary Brooksbank.
Collected by Maurice Fleming.

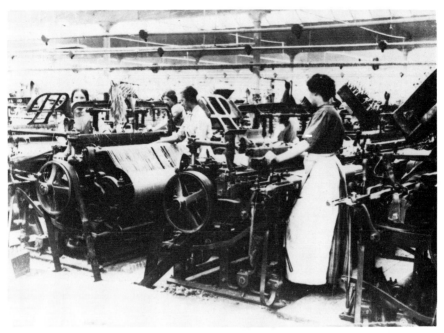

15. Weaving shed at Baxter Bros. mill.

38. THE JUTE MILL SONG

1. Oh, dear me, the mill's gaen fast, The puir wee shifters canna get their rest, Shiftin' bobbins, coorse and fine, They fairly mak' ye work for your ten and nine.

2. Oh, dear me, I wish the day was done, Rinnin' up and doon the pass is no nae fun; Shiftin', piecin', spinning', warp weft and twine, Tae feed and cled my bairnie affen ten and nine.

3. Oh, dear me, the warld's ill-di-vided, Them that work the hardest are aye wi' least pro-vided, But I maun bide contented, dark days or fine, There's nae much pleasure living affen ten and nine.

Written by Mary Brooksbank.
As sung by Mary Brooksbank.
Collected by Maurice Fleming.

84

39. TIRED O' WORKIN

CHORUS: Cox's, Halley's, Eagle, Craigie, Brochie's, Baxter's, Bowbrig, Cairds;

I am getting tired o' workin, But tae lose my job I'm feared.

1. 'Mang the noise o' wheels in motion,
   In a dark unhealthy den;
   Heaven's bricht sky shines here never,
   Clouds o' dust eternal reign.

2. Change of scene the hert may lichten,
   But for us there is nae change;
   Belts and pulleys aye revolvin,
   Where the weary eye may range.

   Chorus

3. Forced tae toil for bare subsistence,
   Scorned by those wha's wealth we've made;
   Even stands insults fae gaffers,
   For the chance tae earn wir bread.

4. Let a worker, though he's richt,
   Dare dispute an overseer;
   Quick he's telt, 'Your service, laddie,
   Is nae langer needed here.'

   Chorus
   Cox's, Halley's, Eagle, Craigie,
   Brochie's, Baxter's, Browbrig, Caird's;
   I am getting tired o' workin,
   But tae lose ma job I'm feared.

Words and music by Jim Reid, Dundee.

85

16. Weaving machinery at Baxter Bros. mill.

40. AULD MAID IN A GARRET

1. Noo I've often heard it said, frae my faither to my mother, Tae gang tae a wedding Was the makin's o' anither, If this be true then I'll gang wi'oot a bidding, Oh, kind providence, will ye tak' me tae a weddin',

CHORUS: For it's oh, dear me, What will I dae, If I dee an auld maid in a garret.

2. Oh my young sister Jean,
   She's no handsome or good-lookin,
   She wis scarcely sixteen
   When puir lassie she wis tooken,
   Noo she's twenty one wi a son and a dochter,
   And I'm forty fower an' I've never had an offer.

3. I can cook and I can sew,
   I can keep a hoose fell tidy,
   Rise early in the moarnin
   An' mak' the breakfast riddy.
   There's naethin' in this world wid mak me half sae cheery,
   If I only had an auld man tae come an' ca' me dearie.

4. Oh, come tinker, come tailor,
   Come soldier or come sailor,
   Come ony man at a'
   That will tak me frae my faither,
   Come rich man, come puir man, wise man or witty,
   Come ony man ava that will tak me oot o' pity.

5. Oh, I'll awa hame
   If there's naebody heedin,
   Naebody's heedin
   Tae puir wee Annie's pleadin,
   I'll awa hame tae my ain wee garret,
   If I canna get a man, then I'll shairly get a parrot.

As sung by Maureen Rooney, Dundee.

41. BETSY BELL

1. My name is Betsy Bell, in the Overgate I dwell, Nae doot ye'll wonder what I'm seekin' here. But if you wait a wee, my tale I'll tell to thee, It's a tale nae doot ye'll think is unco queer.

2. Now I'm lookin for a lad, he may be guid or bad,
   An' I'm gae'n'a tak the first yin that I see,
   Now he may be young or auld, grey heidit now or bald,
   O but onything wi breeks'll dae for me.

3. Now I went oot the ither nicht an' I met wi Sandy Richt,
   An' he winked at me as I was passin by,
   Now says he, 'Wad ye like romance, wad ye be glad of a chance.'
   Oh says I, 'If you're agreeable so am I.'

4. Now I could wash an' I could clean an' weave an' mend a seam,
   Oh jist as guid as ony ane I ken,
   But it's on the nail I'll hing an' I'll aye get leave tae sing,
   'Oh I wonder what's a-dae wi a' the men.'

5. Oh now ye ken wee Janet Cooke, she drinks jist like a fluke,
   Her age is now oh jist three score an' ten,
   Now for husbands she's had three, is there no a chance for me?
   Oh I wonder what's a-dae wi a' the men.

6. Now when I bocht ma mairriage frock, they thocht it wis a joke,
   They laughed at me an' cheered me, oh ye ken,
   But it's on the nail I've hung until the day I've sung,
   'Oh I wonder what's a-dae wi a the men.'

As sung by Annie Watkins, Dundee.
Collected by Maurice Fleming, arranged by Peter Shepheard.

42. THE SPINNER'S WEDDING A

The gaffer's looking worried, the flett's a' in a steer,

Jessie Brodie's getting mairit an' the morn she'll no be here,

CHORUS: Ha ray a row,—— a daddy, O,—— Ha ray a row,— with a

daddy O,— Ha ray a row a daddy 'O,—— Jessie's gettin' mairit O.—

2nd & LATER VERSES: The helper and the piecer went doon the toon last nicht,

Tae buy their wee bit present, jist tae mak her hame look bricht.

2. The helper and the piecer
   Went doon the toon last nicht,
   Tae buy their wee bit present,
   Jist tae mak her hame look bricht.

3. They bocht a chiny tea set,
   A chanty fu o' saut,
   A bonnie coloured carpet,
   A kettle an' a pot.

4. The shifters they're a-dancin,
   The spinners singin tae,
   The gaffer's standin watchin,
   But there's nothin he can dae.

5. Here's best wishes tae ye lassies,
   Standin at yer spinnin frame,
   May ye aye hae full an' plenty,
   In yer wee bit hame.

6. Ye'll no mak muckle siller,
   Nae maitter hoo ye try,
   But hoard ye love an' loyalty,
   That's what money canna buy.

Words and music; Mary Brooksbank.
As sung by Mary Brooksbank.
Collected by Maurice Fleming.

THE SPINNER'S WEDDING B

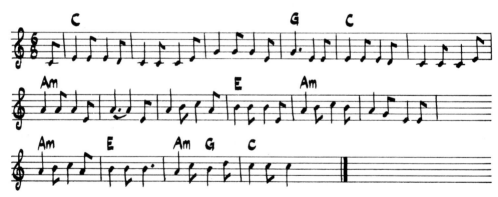

As sung by Ray Fisher.

43. JOHNNY SHAW'S A DECENT CHAP

1. Oh, Johnny Shaw's a decent chap, an' he wants tae mairry me,

An' tho' he's only a cairter chiel he's fourteen bob you see;

Noo I'm awfu' fond o' Johnny for he has such kindly ways,

But when I think o' takin' him his pair auld mither says;

CHORUS: 'Ye can tak' him if ye like an' dae the best ye can,

But never be a safter when ye're dealing wi' a man;

For it's aft times different when he's in a steady job,

But ye'll never be a Lady aff his fourteen bob'.

2. Johnny says if he gets wed an' a family he'll have five,
   We'll hae tae live on sawdust for tae keep them a' alive,
   Johnny says what e'er he gets he'll get it clean an' neat,
   For he can get them meat tae eat an' I can lick the plate.

   'Ye can tak him if ye like an' dae the best ye can,
   But never be a safter when ye're dealin' wi' a man,
   For it's aft times different when he's in a steady job,
   But ye'll never be a lady aff his fourteen bob.'

As sung by Mary Brooksbank.
Collected by Maurice Fleming.

44. THE STRIKE SONG

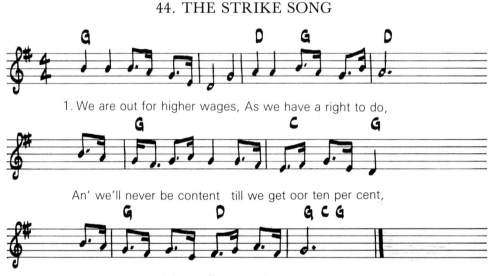

1. We are out for higher wages, As we have a right to do,

An' we'll never be content   till we get oor ten per cent,

For we have a right tae live as well as you.

As sung by Mary Brooksbank.
Collected by Maurice Fleming.

45. THE BUREAU A

1. We're the lads fae the tap o' the hill, We never worked, we never will,

We're on the Bureau, Just like the lads fae Peddie Street, Mention work —

We tak tae oor feet, We're on the Bureau. We got a job in the boatyaird at

the platin', Now that's a job ye've got tae get a stake in, For we stood

on a plank that wasnae there, We went flyin' through the air,

Boatyaird, bye, bye!

2. We're the lads fae Mid Craigie,
   Whaur there's work ye'll no see me,
   We're on the Bureau,
   We're the lads fae the Gelly Burn,
   If we see work we'll dae a wee turn,
   We're on the Bureau.
   We got a job wi Wullie Lang the bookie,
   Collectin lines at the corner o' St Rookie;
   We gied oor clients ower much sub,
   We spent the rest in John o' Groat's pub,
   Bookies, bye bye!

3. We're the lads fae Mid Kirk Style,
   If we see work we'll run for a mile,
   We're on the Bureau.
   We're the lads fae Mid Craigie,
   Whaur there's work ye'll no see me,
   We're on the Bureau.
   We got a job at the cann'ry cannin herrin,
   We sang that sang 'Oor Maggie had a Bairn',
   But the gaffer didna like that sang,
   The job didna rin for verra lang,
   Cann'ries, bye bye!

4. We're the lads fae Mid Craigie,
   Whaur there's work ye'll no see me,
   We're on the Bureau.
   We're the lads fae Mid Kirk Style,
   If we see work, we'll rin for a mile,
   We're on the Bureau.
   We got a job in Walker's at the spinnin,
   But when we saw the frames we started rinnin,
   We're a' the same up tap o' the hill,
   Show us a tool an' we rin like Hell,
   Walker's bye, bye!

5. We're the lads fae the tap o' the hill,
   We never worked, we never will,
   We're on the Bureau.
   We're the lads fae Norrie's Pend,
   We never work an' we don't intend,
   We're on the Bureau.
   We went doon ae Thursday for oor money,
   The cash clerk said, 'Noo, lads youse think your're funny,
   You're oot o' here ye see,
   For noo ye're on the U.A.B.'
   Bureau, bye, bye!

From Alec Clark's singing.
Collected by Maurice Fleming.

17. John o' Groats pub, where the subject of 'The Bureau' spent his income.

THE BUREAU B

1. Now we're the lads fae the tap o' the hill,
   We never worked an' we never will,
   Bye, bye Boab Allan,
   Now we're the lads fae Norrie's Pend,
   We never worked an' we don't intend,
   Bye, bye, Boab Allan.
   When we get oor tickets for the berries,
   We jist toddle doon tae Broughty Ferry,
   We're no on the Parish or the broo,
   We're a' lined up for the grubber noo,
   Boab Allan, bye, bye!

2. Now Allan's just a fly old man,
   Try tae cheat him if ye can,
   Bye, bye, Boab Allan,
   And when he sees you trying to shirk,
   He sends you ootside lookin' for work,
   Bye, bye, Boab Allan.
   But when he gies you a job ye have tae stick it,
   Now don't you think you're gaun tae get a ticket,
   But when he hands me that green caird,
   Oh, I'll tell him I'm no feared,
   Boab Allan, bye, bye!

From the singing of Annie Watkins.
Collected by Maurice Fleming.

95

37. THE DUNDEE LASSIE

Written by Mary Brooksbank, recorded by Maurice Fleming.

The song gives a picture of a cheerful lass, and it is known that the Dundee mill girls had a reputation for their 'hilarity and making light of things'. William Walker, in his book *Juteopolis,* suggests that while this may have been 'whistling in the dark', it was more likely to have been a 'triumph of fortitude over adversity', as there was little for many people in Dundee to be cheerful about, including those lucky enough to have a job.

Often, 'The Dundee Lassie' is sung to the tune of 'The Bonnie Lass o' Fyvie'.

38. THE JUTE MILL SONG

Written by Mary Brooksbank, recorded by Maurice Fleming.

Shifting, piecing and spinning were three jobs of work on the *flett* – the platform on which the spinning machinery stood. The shifter was the person who removed full bobbins from the spinning frames and replaced them with empty ones. These workers were also called *doffers,* and there is an excellent song from the north of England called 'Doffing Mistress'.

Some parts of this song are likely to have been taken from an older song. Charlie Lamb heard from his father that 'ten and nine' was the pay rate for jute workers before the First World War, in the form of a gold half-sovereign and nine pence.

Mary can be heard singing this song on the L.P. 'Festival at Blairgowrie', Topic 12T181.

39. TIRED O' WORKIN

From Jim Reid, recorded by Peter Shepheard. This song started out as a poem in 'Lays and Lyrics from the Factory' by David Carnegie (1878). The original poem referred to mills in Arbroath, but Jim rewrote the words and composed the tune.

Although wages and working conditions in the mill were appalling, unemployment was worse, and anyone raising a voice in protest might find himself out of a job. As the Depression of the '30s took hold, foremen could pick and choose which workers would be employed. Often the politics of the hopeful employee were taken into consideration by the gaffer, leading to the rejection of the more outspoken workers.

All the names in the chorus were those of jute mills, now mostly gone, although many of the names can be recognised in landmarks throughout the city of Dundee. It is ironic that despite the degree of poverty and low wages, it was very fashionable for the owners of the mills, who had made vast fortunes themselves, to give generous donations to the community. Cox's of Lochee donated Camperdown Park and built the swimming pool and library in Lochee. Elsewhere there is Baxter Park and Caird Park.

40. AULD MAID IN A GARRET

From the singing of Maureen Rooney of Charleston, Dundee.

This song is probably not from Dundee originally, as there are variants from all over Britain. There is even an American song called 'The Old Maid's Song' which has a different tune, but it is clear that the roots are the same:

> Come a landsman, a pinsman, a tinker or a tailor,
> A fiddler or a dancer, a ploughboy or a sailor,
> A gentleman, a poor man, a fool or a witty,
> Don't you let me die an old maid, but take me out of pity.

All the variants can possibly be traced back to the seventeenth century, to a broadside ballad called 'The Wooing Maid' by Martin Parker of London, in which the chorus is, 'Come gentle, come simple, come foolish, come witty, Oh, if ye lack a maid, take me for pity'.

However, in spite of the general currency of the song, there was probably no town which related to the words as much as Dundee. Because of the dominance of women in the jute industry, many men were forced to leave Dundee in search of work, and the 1914-18 War contributed even further to the lack of eligible men. Spinsterhood, therefore, was a very real prospect facing many women, and it is easy to see why 'Auld Maid in a Garret' was so popular in Dundee. Even today, many Dundonians feel that it is as much a Dundee song as any other, and most of the versions of the song in the School of Scottish Studies' massive archive of Scots song are from the Dundee and Angus area. The Poets' Box also had a slightly different version.

41. BETSY BELL

From the singing of Annie Watkins, recorded by Maurice Fleming.

Similar in theme to 'Auld Maid in a Garret', this song would have been at one time very popular throughout Scotland. Jeannie Robertson used to sing 'O, my name is Betsy Bell in the *Gallowgate* I dwell' in a Glasgow version of the song, and according to Ray Fisher, 'she'd pick out some poor, innocent male listener and sing directly to him, and he would blush with embarassment'. The Poets' Box also had a lengthy version. Belle Stewart also helped to make this song popular.

42. THE SPINNER'S WEDDING

By Mary Brooksbank, recorded by Maurice Fleming.

Because of the shortage of men in Dundee, there was great excitement in the mill when somebody was going to get married. Her fellow workers would club together and buy a small present, and one of the items featured amongst the wedding gifts was a chamber pot full of salt with a small doll stuck into the salt (see verse two), presumably symbolising wealth and fertility. Even today in Dundee offices and factories the custom is to dress the bride-to-be in an old lace curtain with a stick of rhubarb for a bouquet. Another girl impersonates the bridegroom and the wedding party, complete with baby, parades the streets.

43. JOHNNY SHAW'S A DECENT CHAP

Recorded from Mary Brooksbank, recorded by Maurice Fleming.

The 'fourteen bob' talked about in the song is either the carter's wages, or possibly unemployment benefit. It is also possible that the song is Mary Brooksbank's own composition, as her first experience of political strife was during the Carters' Strike of 1911, and as 'a barefoot wee lassie' she was fascinated by a procession of marching men singing 'The Red Flag'.

44. THE STRIKE SONG

Recorded from Mary Brooksbank by Maurice Fleming.

It is easy to imagine Mary Brooksbank leading the singing of this song during a strike. She first went on strike in 1912, when she learned her 'first lesson in class warfare'. She became more and more politically aware as time went on, and served prison sentences for breach of the peace, and took part in hunger marches and strikes for better wages and conditions. The unemployment situation in the jute industry gave rise to incidents of civil unrest in Dundee. In 1921, after three days of rioting, the Parish Council granted relief benefits without the usual investigations and interviews. In 1923, when 30,000 workers were locked out after striking, the jobless total rose to half the working population. 50,000 people gathered in Albert Square to demonstrate, which led to more street violence. In 1931 there were more unemployment demonstrations and more arrests.

Mary Brooksbank must have based her rhyme on an older song. A song about a Dock strike in London during the 1880s has the chorus:

> Strike boys, strike for better wages,
> Strike boys, strike for better pay.
> Go on fighting at the docks, Stick it out like fighting cocks,
> Go on fighting 'till the bosses they give way.

45. THE BUREAU

A) Based on a version collected from Alec Clark of Dundee by Maurice Fleming. The tune is 'Bye Bye Blackbird'.

This song was possibly more widespread in Scotland during the Depression, as there still exists in Glasgow a rhyme which goes, 'I'm Buffalo Bill fi Maryhill, I've never worked an' I never will'. However, it is in Dundee that the only versions of it are recorded. The John O'Groats public house stood at the corner of the Cowgate and St. Roques Lane (St. Rookie). The 'Bureau' was the Bureau of Employment, commonly known as 'the broo'. Benefit could only be drawn at the 'Bureau' for a certain period of unemployment, depending on stamps paid while in work. After they had 'run out', an unemployed person then had to depend on the U.A.B. – the Unemployment Assistance Board, or 'the Parish' – hence the last line of the song, 'Bureau, bye, bye!'

B) Based on a version from Annie Watkins recorded by Peter Shepheard.

Boab Allan was the Parish Council Officer. The 'tickets fur the berries' may have been paid for by the parish so that the employed jute workers could get jobs picking berries. Dundee is at the centre of the largest raspberry-growing area in Scotland, which still provides seasonal employment for many people. The 'grubber' was the poorhouse.

98

Dundee Worthies

Every town of reasonable size had its 'worthies', characters who were in one way or another outwith the norm. They would include itinerant street singers, like Blin' Hughie, button sellers, pie sellers, and also more ordinary people who either had an exuberant outlook upon life or merely had the misfortune to be disfigured or epileptic. Worthies were generally well thought of, and there are books and numerous songs celebrating the antics of the Dundee worthies.

The most famous of all the Dundee worthies was the self-styled 'poet and tragedian', William Topaz McGonagall, known throughout the world as 'the only truly memorable bad poet in our language'. McGonagall believed in his own genius, seeing himself as being as great as Shakespeare and Burns. His remarkable talent was to some extent recognised in his own day – most of his poetry was published, and he performed in front of paying audiences, not accepting that their mock adulation was anything but genuine praise. In the streets, people would shout after him 'There goes Mad McGonagall' and hurl stones and snowballs at him, and when he announced his intention to leave Dundee to escape the 'ignorant rabble', a poem appeared in the *Weekly News* welcoming the announcement, and ridiculing the poet's appearance, especially his long hair. McGonagall replied in verse:

> . . . in conclusion, I'd have him to beware,
> And never again to interfere with a poet's hair,
> Because Christ the Saviour wore long hair,
> And many more good men, I do declare.

Throughout all this ridicule, McGonagall still believed in himself as a great poetic genius who would one day be crowned with the laurels of fame. People from all over the world today celebrate McGonagall's poetry as having a mysterious, comical fascination in its sincerity, and he still stands today as the most memorable of all Dundee's characters.

46. BLIN' HUGHIE

1. Wha hasna heard tell o' Blin' Hughie the singer?
   The last wandering minstrel o' Scottish sang-lore;
   I'm sure in some mem'ries his ootlines still linger,
   For worthy was Hughie o' fouk to adore.
   His lang, strappin' figure was crooned wi' a bannet,
   A real Kilmarnock o' weatherproof blue,
   That, like a corona encircling a planet,
   Hung wi' its red toorie ahint to the view.

2. His bonnie broo bare to the sun and the weather,
   Surmounted in beauty his life-darkened een;
   His coothie-like face, wi the hue o' hairst heather,
   Made ilka observer o' Hughie a freen.
   His broon vocal thrapple was void o' a' happin,
   His strippet sark collar hung doon in twa peaks;
   His short furzy coat was the warmest o' wrappin,
   Weel buttoned ower waistcoat an' corduroy breeks.

3. His shoon, wi their soles tacket-studded and clampit,
   Defied ilka leather-made fashion or mode;
   But Hughie ne'er heeded sae lang as he trampit
   Dry shod ower the miles o' ilk rough Scottish road.
   A staff he aye carried, wi its handle-en' crookit,
   To be his sole guide; hech! 'twas nae use ava;
   For somehoo or ither his feelin' aye lookit,
   An' guardit him weel frae a gutter or wa'.

4. The crook o' his staff ower his wrist-bane aye hingin,
   His thochtfu'-like face lookin doon tae the grun,
   Wi mou a wee thrawn-ways Hugh startit his singin,
   An' peered fu appealingly up to the sun.
   He'd sing o' the Stuarts, an' hielan devotion,
   He'd sing o' the tartan, the mountain and heath,
   He felt what he sang, sae, owercome wi emotion,
   His hearers wad sab wi a faltering breath.

5. Ilk market an' fair tint the haif o' its pleasure
   Gin Hughie was no in the thick o' the thrang,
   Delightin the lassies wi some hinny measure,
   Or firin the chiels wi a heart-grippin' sang.
   The hame-ower, pathetic, their joys was be calmin,
   Love ditties, lane courtin's, wad kittle ilk heart;
   But wi 'Came Ye By Athol' he'd droon Robbie Salmon,
   The eloquent gingerbread man, an' his cart.

6. Puir Robbie wad start a lang-windit oration
   (An' better than he we'll nae mair see at fairs),
   Yet a' heard the finish o' Hugh's emanations,
   Ere ever they'd gang to buy gingerbread wares.
   Nae mair we'll hear Hughie, wi voice ringin cheerie,
   Nae mair will he warble the soul-rousing strain;
   He sees an' sings in the hame for the weary,
   An' Scotland will greet for her true-hearted wean.

18. Blin' Hughie.

47. JENNY MARSHALL'S CANDY O

1. When going along the Nethergate, There's naught can be so handy, O,

As drapping in to get a stick of Jenny Marshall's candy, O.

CHORUS: Oh, Jenny Marshall, Jenny Marshall, Jenny Marshall's candy, O,

I always like to patronise Jenny Marshall's candy, O.

2. Ye'll get a stick as streicht's a rash,
A crookit ane or bandy, O,
The grandest treat for little cash
Is Jenny Marshall's candy O.

3. The ladies fine come in the street,
Wi' dresses a'fu dandy, O,
And weel they like their mou's to weet
Wi' Jenny Marshall's candy O.

4. There's no' a lass in a' Dundee,
Frae modest dame to randy, O,
But wha wad want her cup o' tea
For Jenny Marshall's candy O.

5. There's no' a loon in a' the toon,
A Jamie or a Sandy, O,
But wha wad want his piece at noon
For Jenny Marshall's candy O.

6. When weety winter wi the hoast
Is like to reive and rend ye, O,
The best o' cures at little cost
Is Jenny Marshall's candy O.

7. Some uses draps o' peppermint
   To kill the smell o' brandy, O,
   But, by my shuith, I'm weel content
   Wi' Jenny Marshall's candy O.

8. Then come awa baith great an' sma,
   An' let your purse attend ye, O,
   And, while ye find a baubie in't,
   Buy Jenny Marshall's candy O.

48. WORTHIES OF DUNDEE I

1. It's noo, my lads, I'll sing a sang,
   An' sure I am it's new,
   Although the characters I'll name
   Hae lang been kent by you.
   There's first Pie Jock, syne Jeely Heel,
   Then Hairy Kail at shore,
   Wi Chaw Nails too, an' Charlie Gray,
   Two lads that drink galore.

   Chorus:
   Yet fam'd tho' these may be in toon,
   Pie Jock still dings them a';
   For he's been up an' roon the moon,
   Like John o' Arran Ha'.

2. Noo see the Jolly Beggar, low
   Wi snack mou in his throat,
   Wi Troaky Nose an' Docherty,
   His face as clean's the pot;
   Then Davie Rait an' Sandy Young,
   An' Frazer, oor gude drummer,
   Wi Pie Snap too, and Fussie Gow,
   An' Fire, the ill-tongued limmer.

3. There's Singin Hughie, he comes next,
   'Mang singers he's a king,
   Then Cadger Jamie Williamson,
   Wi haddocks, cod, or ling;
   Syne Bob Watt, bawlin' dilse an' tangle,
   An' new boiled wilks a treat;
   Wi Coffin Blake perched on his box,
   Deck'd in cravat an' cape.

4. Then Piper Simpson comes by chance,
   An' up his bags he blaws,
   Till Tailor Third gets up to dance,
   But's seized by Gashie Tawse.
   Next in the fray comes Jamie May,
   Wi funny Andrew Buddie;
   An' by and by, the sweep-lum Dye,
   Wi Saut an' Whitin's cuddie.

5. Nae doot this sang is somewhat long,
   But yet before I close,
   I hae twa ither characters
   O' which I maun dispose –
   Then Stormonth comes, the auctioneer,
   O'Farrel comes an' a';
   An' if Auld Horny wants a leear,
   Dundee can furnish twa!

49. FIZZY GOW'S TEA PARTY

1. Kind freens I'm here again, I've just come out afore ye,
   To sing anither sang, 'cause ye kindly did encore me.
   I like to see ye a' my freens, sae smiling gay and hearty,
   The sang I'm gaun to sing to you is 'Fizzy Gow's Tea Party'.

   Chorus:
   Lall a dall a dae, Lall a dall a dae,
   What fall a daddy fall a dall a dae.

2. Now the pairty it was held in the holy land o' Fish Street,
   Fish heads and tatties, Athol pies and pig's feet,
   Fire's Nanny she came in, swore she wad cook Cow Heel's goose,
   And Hairy Kail cam' rinnin' in, he'd hooked it frae the Poorhoose.

3. Now they called on Hughie for a song,
   To keep the pairty rinnin long,
   When Mag Gow she got up a knife, an' swore she'd stab Auld Andra Buddy,
   She missed the mark, the knife run in the tail o' Fizzy's cuddy.

4. Now Fizzy swore by the death o' his auld cuddy,
   And for 'The Razor' tae the dock they sent off Andra Buddy,
   And when the Razor he came in, Waterloo he wasna hearty,
   And him and Mag got sixty days ower Fizzy Gow's Tea Party.

19. Fish Street, home of many Dundee worthies.

50. CADGERS O' DUNDEE

1. Among some cadgers o' Dundee, An awfu' row began, Between brave Charlie Perrie, and famous Honey Tam, Tam seized the knife for cutting cheese, And he went down on his bended knees, And swore by Lord Dundreary, That it's as sure's my name is Honey Tam, And as sure as I stop up in the Holy Land, I'll murder Charlie Perrie.

2. Alang Fish Street he ran, and he met wi Mattie Big Toe.
   'Did you see whaur Charlie Perrie's gane?', but Mattie answered no.
   Mattie cried, 'You're awfu cheery';
   He kissed the blade o' the big cheese knife,
   And swore by a' that's dreary,
   'This very night before I sleep,
   I'll hae my victim at my feet,
   My victim Charlie Perrie.'

3. When Charlie heard o' this, alang Fish Street he ran,
   And he seized a haud o' Tammas, an' the wrestlin then began,
   Charlie cries, 'Will ye no gie in?'
   'Na, na,' cries Tammas, 'till the row is a' dune,'
   And the nicht being dark and dreary,
   Charlie nails Tam between the een,
   And loudly out bold Tammas cries,
   'Yer the winning man, Charlie Perrie.'

106

51. INDYGO BLUE

1. Kind freens if ye listen a while tae me,
   I'll sing tae ye of a chap in Dundee.
   I'm sure ye'll a' ken him, when his name I tell to you,
   The king ower the bairns was Indygo Blue.

   Chorus:
   Oh, Indygo Blue! Oh, Indygo Blue!
   He goes round the middens for an auld boot or shoe,
   Oh pity the hardships of Indygo Blue.

2. The first time I saw him, was at the West Port,
   Wi a lot o' wee bairns, o' him they made sport,
   He up wi his stick and a lamp it went through,
   Highland Donald he lifted poor Indygo Blue.

3. Early next morning in the court he did stand,
   Wi' a bag on his back and a stick in his hand,
   Says the Bailie to Indygo, that conduct won't do,
   So ten days to prison went Indygo Blue.

4. When the turnkey saw him, he couldna but laugh,
   He says, come awa Indygo till you get your bath,
   The bag frae his back on the floor then he threw,
   And headlong into the water went Indygo Blue.

5. He goes round the rag stores and a' that he steals,
   He tries for to blame it on poor Bag o' Nails;
   Bag up wi' his hand and struck him one in the mou;
   And down through a siver went Indygo Blue.

52. DONAL DON

1. Wha hasna heard o' Donal' Don, Wi' a' his tanterwallops on,

For oh, he was a lazy drone, And smuggled hielan' whisky.

2. When first he cam tae auld Dundee
   'Twas in a smeeky hole lived he;
   Where gauger bodies couldna see,
   He played the king a pliskie.

3. When he was young and in his prime,
   He loo'ed a bonnie lassie fine;
   She jilted him an' aye sin syne
   He's dismal, dull and dusky.

4. A bunch o' rags is a' his braws,
   His heathery wig wad fricht the craws;
   His dusky face and clorty paws
   Wad fyle the Bay of Biscay.

5. He has a sark, he has but ane,
   It's fairly worn tae skin an' bane,
   A loupin, like tae rin its lane
   Wi troopers bauld and frisky.

6. Whene'er his sark's laid oot tae dry
   It's Donald in his bed maun lie,
   An' wait till a' the troopers die,
   Ere he gangs oot wi whisky.

7. So here's a health tae Donal Don,
   Wi a' his tanterwallops on,
   An' may he never lack a scone
   While he maks Hielan' whisky.

53. BLIND MATTIE

1. Just a box of old buttons tired and worn, That ne'er fastened shirt, coat or shoon; It wis played by a dame, Blind Mattie's her name, As she sang aroond old Dundee town. CHORUS: Squeeze the old squeeze box an' rattle the can, Never mindin the wind or the rain; Though the nichts are drawin in an' the blood's gettin thin, It's time tae be singin a — gain.

2. At markets and fairs, and roond the back stairs,
   Her songs could be heard sweet an' shrill;
   Count Your Blessings, Ma Ain Folk, Dark Lochnagar,
   And *The Old Rustic Bridge by the Mill.*

3. 'Count your blessings,' she sang, in her dark world it rang,
   Though blessings were few in her life;
   They were there a' the same in courage and fame,
   And a wit that wis sharp as a knife.

4. She'd tell ye wi glee, teetotal wis she,
   And at them that believed her she'd grin;
   For to see her day through, she liked tea it's true,
   Just as lang as dark rum wis poured in.

5. The melodeon she played in a glass case is laid,
   Wi a picture o' Mattie hersel;
   Sma-bouket an' wee, battered box on her knee
   But if you look close you can tell . . .

109

Final Chorus:
Though the hands on the buttons are crooked with age,
The shoulders a' burdened wi care;
The hair may be white, but the spirit and flight
That she showed a' her days is still there.

(Repeat first Chorus)

Words and Music by Stewart Brown.

54. WORTHIES OF DUNDEE II

Sung to the tune of 'The Bonnets of Bonnie Dundee' (No. 10)

1. Ae nicht feelin drowsy I had a bit stroll,
   As far as the Provie wi auld Willie Croll;
   We went intae the Stag on oor road comin back,
   Just tae hae a bit song or a wee social crack.
   Big Peter the tinky wis there playin jigs,
   Fidgy Mick he wis waltzin wi twa Glesca prigs;
   But when Auld Davie Shinem he jined in the dance,
   Poet McGonagall hadna the ghost o' a chance.

2. Honey Tam an' Gowk Lowden were dressed tae some tune,
   Likewise Fizzy Gow and the famous Muldoon;
   Geordie Tasker, Dulse Charlie an' Big Candy Bob,
   Were discussin home rule wi the great Sandy Robb.
   Mattie Big Toe the Snooser, Fly, Mick and Blue Jock,
   Were there wi Match Patty an' auld Cheeky Rock;
   Coo Heel bein chairman who felt rather big,
   Proposed Donald Blue for a guid Irish jig.

3. Peter screwed up his drones tae the tune o' *Quick Time*
   When the jiggin and dancin wis somethin sublime;
   Then the chairman cries oot, 'It's McGonagall's turn,
   For his noble recital o' famed *Bannockburn.*'
   Blind Hughie rose up gave his mooth a bit traw,
   He sang *Auld Robin Gray* an' *Ma Nannie's Awa,*
   And Auld David the fiddler he's a man that's no blate,
   Gave them a bit stave o' *Oor Little Kate.*

4. They got mixter maxter an' kicked up a row,
   An' Shinem he scattered the great Fizzy Gow;
   Honey Tam and Gowk Lowden got clear o' the scrape,
   But the tinky's physog wis knocked clean oot o' shape.
   The fech o' the worthies has lang passed awa,
   They fear nae the cauld blast, the drift, nor the snaw;
   On oor street, lane or market nae mair ye will see,
   Those auld fashioned worthies o' Bonnie Dundee.

As sung by Jim Reid, Dundee.

110

55. LOCHEE

1. By dark Lochee's lanes and lochs, Sheepskin burns and waterin trochs,

Whaur candy-men deal in rags an' banes, And the streets are no a' paved wi

cassie stanes; Tattie engines, ice-cream stands, Organ grinders an' German

bands, Butchers, bakers, undertakers, Umbrella fakirs and weekly pawns,

Polismen wi big flet feet, Walkin up an' doon the giddy village street,

Baillie Perrie's kingdom is sweet, Here's my respects tae Lochee.

  2. Oh, Lochee I loe that name, Oh, Lochee my native hame,
   Whaur there each day instead o' lookin for work,
   I gang an' play at fitba in the Lochee Park;
   'Twas in that park I first fell in,
   With a lassie wi a pimple on her chin,
   My wee fairy, pie-faced Mary,
   She lived in Tipperary wi a man ca'd Flynn;
   Hawkin sticks or sellin sand,
   Here's ma fit, there's a blister on ma hand,
   God save the Queen an' St Margaret's old brass band,
   Here's my respects tae Lochee.

Words and music by William Harkins, Lochee.
As sung by Charlie Lamb, Lochee.
Recorded by Maurice Fleming.

111

56. STOBBIE PARLIAMENT PICNIC

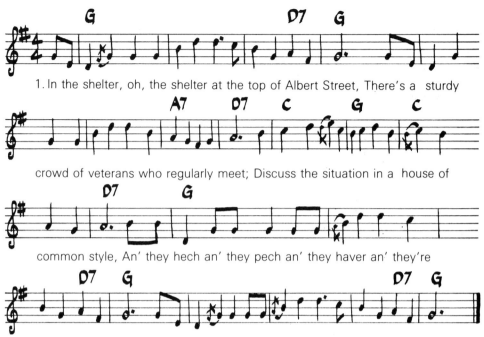

1. In the shelter, oh, the shelter at the top of Albert Street, There's a sturdy crowd of veterans who regularly meet; Discuss the situation in a house of common style, An' they hech an' they pech an' they haver an' they're happy a' the while. Wi ma fal lal lal di ma ral di dal, Ma fal lal lal di day.

2. Ae day while hot the bet was on, Jamie Reid cam near,
   'I think we'll organise a drive while summer days are hear.'
   The auld lads said it wad be great the countryside tae see,
   Says Jamie, 'I'll get oot the brake, just leave it up tae me.'

3. The plan was soon adopted and arrangements duly made,
   Whereby the outin wad take place and a' expenses paid.
   There was fellowship and freedom and refreshments beyond praise,
   'Twas the rarest and the fairest and the merriest of days.

4. He drove the brake tae Tullybaccart and Kinclaven Bridge,
   Whaur they had a marvelous picnic on dismounting from the rig;
   The weather was sae kind to them, the sun shone a' the while,
   The return journey took them roon by Meigle and Newtyle.

5. So come a' ye that's gaithered here tae welcome them a' hame,
   This trip has gained intself a place in Stobbie's hall of fame;
   An' while ye're cheering ane an' a' just let me hear your cries
   Of thanks for Jamie Reid's horse brake and Durkie's tasty pies.

Words and music by Jim Reid.
Reprinted by permission of Springthyme Music.

46. BLIN' HUGHIE

From the Poets' Box, called 'Blin' Hughie of Dundee, The Ballad Singer'. No tune given.

Blin' Hughie was one of the most popular street singers of his day, famed for his joviality, his scrupulous honesty and his clear, strong voice. His real name was either Hugh Lennox or Hugh M. Gowans, and he died in Dundee in the 1880s.

A report of Hughie's appearance went like this: '. . . his stout burly figure stood as erect as a post. His hat thrown well back on his head showed his broad gauchy face turned to the sky. He always carried a walking stick, and when he began his entertainment he hung the staff by the crook over his left arm. His body twisted in grotesque contortions, shrugging his shoulders and hitching up his trousers as he carolled forth his songs in a style peculiarly his own'.

It was said that Hughie seemed 'intensely happy when rolling off some laughable song or ballad', and it would appear that his best remembered performances were of comic songs. At one time in Scotland there were popular songs and rhymes which gave lists of items sold in general stores. Blin' Hughie used to sing a parody of this type of song, with verse after verse of ridiculous goods to be had at a fictitious store. The song was called 'Good News', and among the items for sale were 'Razor straps and curling stanes, Epsom Salts and wheelbarrows, Wine grapes and potato graips, Mason's mells and gum flowers'.

47. JENNY MARSHALL'S CANDY O

From *Dundee Worthies* by George Martin (1934), the tune given being 'I'm Ower Young'.

Blin' Hughie used to sing this song in the streets of Dundee. It was written by Robert Leighton (1822-69), a Dundee merchant who published several volumes of poetry during his lifetime, and whose better-known songs include 'My Muckle Meal Pock' and 'Spunk Janet's Cure for Love'. Jenny Marshall had a sweet shop in the Nethergate which was patronised by the 'lads and lasses on the summer evenings'. After Leighton wrote the song, there is a story about Jenny Marshall not being very happy about it, and consulting a lawyer to see if she could get 'that loon Bob Leighton punished for his impudence'.

48. WORTHIES OF DUNDEE I

This song is from a Poets' Box sheet, but it was also published in the 1930s book *Dundee Worthies* by George Martin, which was full of reminiscences and descriptions of characters and pastimes of the nineteenth century. The hero of the song appears to be 'Pie Jock', a hawker of Dundee. His real name was John Fergusson, and he was a short, lopsided figure of a man. Pie Jock sold household items during the day and pies in the evening, carrying a hot pie oven strapped over his shoulder. His 'Pies! Hot pies!' cry was familiar throughout Dundee, but even years after he had stopped selling pies he was still known as Pie Jock. In common with other worthies, he would be prey to the children in the street, who would sing songs such as:

> Pie Jock beats them a'
> For he's been up and around the moon
> Wi' John o' Arnha'.

Also in common with other worthies, Pie Jock was fond of a drink now and again, and he is mentioned in a lengthy poem by 'F.W.S.':

> These twa worthies had a booze,
> Pie Jock he wanted hame,
> And through the clouds came tumbling down
> And landed in Trades Lane.

Among the other worthies mentioned in the song are 'Jeely Heel', a butcher's messenger whose real name was Willie Morris. He seems to have been remembered affectionately as, after his death, a wax effigy of him was exhibited in a show in the Overgate. Another was 'Hairy Kail', whose nickname came from an incident in which he stuffed a live cat into his mother's boiling kail pot. On her return he told her, 'Hairy kail the day, mother, hairy kail the day'. Troaky Nose was a harbour porter and Pie Snap was a character from the Hilltown. 'Fire' or 'Fire Nanny' was a fat, elderly woman who had a shop in the Wellgate. She liked a drink, and when in her cups would attempt to kiss any man she saw. 'Gashie Tawse' was a policeman who was toothless, and the children all called him 'Gashie', much to his annoyance.

49. FIZZY GOW'S TEA PARTY

This was possibly a music-hall song, from the wording of the first verse. Printed in *Dundee Worthies* by George Martin (1934). The 'Holy Land' featured in this song as well as in 'Cadgers o' Dundee' may have been a nickname for Fish Street, or a lodging house there.

50. CADGERS O' DUNDEE

From the Poets' Box. The tune is 'The Battle of Stirling Bridge'.

Cadgers, or barrow vendors, were very common in the eighteenth and nineteenth centuries, and one such fish cadger was called 'Honey Tam'. Tam did business in the Greenmarket, and he was a short, fat man who wore ragged 'moleskins' (heavy, brushed cotton trousers). The children annoyed him by singing 'Oh! my, I'm no' carin', Scabby Joe and Honey Tam are noo sellin' stinkin' herrin'.' Tam was something of an aggressive type, and an incident between him and one of his enemies, Charlie Pirie, or Perrie, gave rise to this song.

51. INDYGO BLUE

From the Poets' Box, no tune given.

Indygo Blue was an itinerant seller of 'blue caum' or 'cam', which was blue camstone, a type of pipe-clay made up into blocks with which housewives used to decorate the stone slabs of their doorsteps. In Glasgow, tenement stairs were washed and then caumed over by Irish women for about 2d per flight. In many places circles of blue caum were drawn on doorsteps to keep the 'wee folk' away. Fishing villages on the Fife coast and Newhaven on the Forth used a lot of this substance on the doorsteps, but used white caum for the hearthstone inside. Because of the blue caum that he sold, Indygo Blue always seemed to have a bright blue face, much to the delight of the Dundee children, and he would walk around the streets singing 'I'm Indy, I'm Indy, I'm Indygo Blue!'

52. DONAL DON

From Robert Ford's *Vagabond Songs and Ballads of Scotland* 1899-1901. The tune is 'Rob Roy's March'.

Scotland's main drink until after the Union of Parliaments in 1707 was ale, and in Dundee one reason for this was the appalling water supply. Even the Church, which preached against spirits, approved of beer as 'strengthening'. Many people objected to the new taxes going to the London Exchequer, as it was regarded as being used to pay English debts, and as a result the smuggling of gin, whisky and rum became widespread. This made spirits cheaper than the taxed ale, and the 'gauger bodies', the customs and excise men, hunted the smugglers with determination. One of the smuggling routes was from Barry, on the Forfarshire coast, to the town of Forfar, and then on to Dundee.

53. BLIND MATTIE

Written by Stewart Brown of the *Lowland Folk* and recorded on their album 'Time to be Singing Again' on Balaena Records BRLP 3001.

When Blind Mattie died, she had been earning a living playing her melodion and singing in the streets of Dundee for seventy years. Her instrument is now in a glass case in Barrack Street Museum, alongside a photograph of Blind Mattie herself. Blind is pronounced in the Scots manner – Blin with d on the end.

54. WORTHIES OF DUNDEE II

As sung by Jim Reid. Words adapted from a set in *Dundee Worthies,* set to the tune of 'The Bonnets o' Bonnie Dundee'.

Another collection of worthies, the same old favourites cropping up again – Fizzy Gow, Mattie Big Toe, Blin' Hughie, Honey Tam and all.

55. LOCHEE

Collected by Maurice Fleming from Charlie Lamb of Lochee. Sung to the tune 'Killarney', this song was composed by William Harkins, another Lochee resident. Baillie Perrie (pronounced Biley Peerie) was a local councillor in Lochee before the First War. He had a boil on his neck and so his name had a double meaning. The Tipperary in the song is not in Ireland, but an area in Lochee near Cox Brothers' jute mill, and was named thus because the area housed immigrant Irish working in the mills.

56. STOBBIE PARLIAMENT PICNIC

Words and Music by Jim Reid. Reprinted with permission of Springthyme music. Recorded by Jim Reid on his album 'I Saw the Wild Geese Flee' (Springthyme SPR 1015). This song was first published around 1908 and rewritten by Jim Reid. It is about the annual picnic outing for the old men and characters of Stobbie (Stobswell), and Jamie Reid in the song was Jim Reid's uncle, who ran the horse-drawn bus from the stables at Stobswell. Durkie's were the forerunners of Wallace's famous 'Land o' Cakes'.

True Love

The love songs of the Scots are as abundant as any other nation's – the love song is as universal as it is ageless. The best of Scottish love songs rank among the world's greatest, and are often simple expressions of emotion which touch us all.

With Burns came a change in the Scottish love song; although Ramsay and other poets of the eighteenth century had started introducing elements of formal poetry into folk-style songs, the sheer popularity of Burns meant that his poetry reached all corners of Scotland and inspired an army of followers to write poetry and song. Thus the nineteenth century saw a remarkable rise in the number of volumes of new Scottish songs, and the best-known of the new writers – Skinner, Tannahill, Hector MacNeill and others – represented literally hundreds of minor poets who put pen to paper in a post-Burnsian enthusiasm, often based on romantic notions of Scotland's history.

Generally, these are love songs of the worst kind. They are over-sentimental and have more to do with the use of flowery language than genuine emotion. This is paralleled in today's pop lyrics, where composers use the form of a love song as an abstract vehicle for the music.

With so many people writing new Scottish-style songs, there came a demand for localised songs from the song printers like Sanderson's in Edinburgh and the Poets' Box in Dundee. The Poets' Box catalogue listed such songs as 'Artful Glasgow Dodger', 'Bonnie Aberdonian', 'My Charming Dundee Nell' (sung to the tune of a Burns song), and 'The Birks of Green Balgay' (obviously sung to the tune 'The Birks of Invermay'). Of the songs in this section, 'Betsy of Dundee', 'Bonnie Broughty Ferry Fisher Lass', 'Rose o' Dundee' and 'Ma Bonnie Wee Lochee Lass' fall into this category.

57. THE BANKS OF SWEET DUNDEE II A

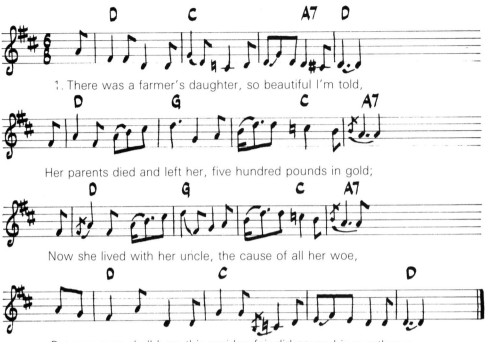

1. There was a farmer's daughter, so beautiful I'm told,

Her parents died and left her, five hundred pounds in gold;

Now she lived with her uncle, the cause of all her woe,

But you soon shall hear this maiden fair did cause his overthrow.

2. Her uncle had a ploughboy young Mary loved full well.
   And in her uncle's garden their tales of love would tell;
   There was a wealthy squire, who oft her came to see,
   But still she loved the ploughboy on the banks of sweet Dundee.

3. 'Twas on a summer's morning her uncle went straightway,
   He knocked on Mary's bedroom door and unto her did say,
   'Come rise up, pretty maiden, a lady you may be,
   The squire is waiting for you on the banks of sweet Dundee.'

4. 'A fig for all your squires, your lords and dukes likewise,
   My William he appears to me like diamonds in my eyes.'
   'Begone, unruly female, you ne'er shall happy be,
   I mean to banish William from the banks of sweet Dundee.'

5. Her uncle and the squire rode out one summer's day,
   'Young William is in favour,' her uncle he did say;
   'Indeed 'tis my intention to tie him to a tree,
   Or else to bribe the press-gang on the banks of sweet Dundee.'

6. The press-gang came to William when he was all alone,
   He bodly fought for liberty, but they were six to one;
   The blood did flow in torrents, 'Pray kill me now', said he,
   'I'd rather die for Mary on the banks of sweet Dundee.'

7. This maid one day was walking, lamenting for her love,
   She met the wealthy squire, down in her uncle's grove,
   He put his arms around her, 'Stand off, base man,' said she,
   'You sent the only lad I love from the banks of sweet Dundee.'

8. He clasped his arms around her, and tried to throw her down,
   Two pistols and a sword she spied beneath his morning gown;
   Young Mary took the pistols, his sword he used so free,
   Then she did fire, and shot the squire, on the banks of sweet Dundee.

9. Her uncle overheard the noise, and hastened to the ground,
   'Oh since you've killed the squire, I'll give you your deathwound.'
   'Stand off, then,' cried Mary, 'Undaunted I will be.'
   She trigger drew, her uncle slew, on the banks of sweet Dundee.

10. A doctor soon was sent for, a man of noted skill,
    Likewise came his lawyer, for him to sign his will;
    He willed the gold to Mary, who fought so manfully,
    Then closed his eyes, no more to rise, on the banks of sweet Dundee.

11. Young William he was sent for, and quickly did return,
    As soon as he came back again, young Mary ceased to mourn.
    The day it was appointed, they joined their hands so free,
    And now they live in splendour on the banks of sweet Dundee.

As sung by Eck Harley.
Collected and arranged by Peter Shepheard.

THE BANKS OF SWEET DUNDEE II B

As sung by Jim Reid.
Arranged by Peter Shepheard.

58. SCOTS CALLAN O' BONNIE DUNDEE

1. O, whaur gat ye that hauver-meal bannock? O, silly blind body, o, dinna ye see? I. gat it frae a brisk sodger laddie Atween Saint Johnstone and Bonnie Dundee! O, gin I saw the laddie that gi'ed me't, Aft has he doudl'd me upon his knee; May heaven protect my bonnie Scots laddie,

And send him safe hame tae his baby and me.

2. My heart has nae room when I think on my laddie,
   His dear rosy haffets bring tears to my ee –
   But O! he's awa, and I dinna ken whaur he's –
   Awa' frae his lassie and Bonnie Dundee.
   O light be the breeze around him saft blawin!
   And o'er him sweet simmer still blink bonnilie,
   And the rich dews o' plenty, around him wide fa'in,
   Prevent a' his fears for his baby and me!

3. My blessings upon that sweet wee lippie!
   My blessings upon that bonnie ee-brie!
   Thy smiles are sae like my blythe sodger laddie,
   Thou's aye the dearer and dearer tae me.
   But I'll big a bower on yon green bank sae bonnie,
   That's lave'd by the waters o' Tay wimplin' clear,
   And cleed thee in tartans, my wee smiling Johnnie,
   And make thee a man like your daddie dear.

Tune as sung by Jim Reid.

120

59. JAMIE FRAE DUNDEE

1. I canno' like ye gentle sir, although a laird ye be, I lo'e a bonny Scottish lad Wha brought me frae Dundee. CHORUS: Had awa' wi' Jamie, Had awa' wi' Jamie, Had awa' wi' Ja—mie o'er the lea, I gang'd along wi' free gude will, He's a' the world to me.

2. I'se gang wi Jamie frae Dundee,
   To cheer the lanesome way,
   His cheeks are ruddy o'er wi health,
   He's frolick as the may.

3. The laverock mounts to hail the morn,
   The lint-white swell her throat,
   But neither are sa sweet, sa clear,
   As Jamie's tunefu note.

60. DONALD O' DUNDEE

1. Young Donald is the blythest lad   That e'er made love to me, Whene'er

he's by, my heart is glad,   He seems so gay and free.

Then on his pipes he plays so sweet, And in his plaid he looks so neat,

It cheers my heart at e'en to meet   Young Donald o' Dundee.

2. Whene'er I gang to yonder grove,
   Young Sandy follows me,
   And fain he wants to be my love,
   But ah! it canna be.
   Though mither frets baith ear' and late
   For me to wed this youth I hate;
   There's nane need hope to gain young Kate
   But Donald o' Dundee.

3. When last we rang'd the banks o' Tay,
   The ring he showed to me;
   And bade me name the bridal day,
   And happy we would be.
   I ken the youth will aye prove kind,
   Nae mair my mither will I mind,
   Mess John to me shall quickly bind
   Young Donald o' Dundee.

61. BETSY O' DUNDEE

1. You sailors of this nation, I pray you give attention, It is no false
in- ven-tion, as plainly you may see; My Parents in this na-tion they live by
culti-vation   In a rural habitation near the banks of sweet Dundee.

2. When young I took the ocean, for riches and promotion,
   With an inclination strange countries for to see;
   But the wars now being over, I was discharged at Dover,
   Then I returned a rover to the banks of sweet Dundee.

3. To ramble I inclined – my parents seldom minded –
   For they by love were blinded and partial unto me.
   Fair maids I always courted – from nymph to nymph resorted;
   My time I spent in courting on the banks of sweet Dundee.

4. Till at length a lovely maid my youthful heart betrayed,
   Beneath the fragrant shade, where I spied that lovely she.
   Without deliberation I asked her habitation;
   In accents sweet she answered me, 'I'm Betsy o' Dundee.'

5. In secret love we courted, while sweet birds round us sported,
   The valleys were our chambers we found the most secure,
   Her father coming by, beneath the shade did spy us,
   And strangely he did use us on the banks of sweet Dundee.

6. He seized this charming fair by the ringlets of the hair,
   She fell into dispair – set my very heart in flame.
   He says – 'I have information you are going to leave this nation,
   And drive to desperation your character and fame.'

7. She said – 'If he had gold we would never be controll'd,
   You would us both enfold with the greatest harmony.
   If it's your determination to cause a separation,
   In spite of all relations with him I'll leave Dundee.'

8. He says – 'If you are inclined, with an honest upright mind,
   This night you shall be joined – so come along with me.'
   What pleasure did surround me, and nuptial bands soon crowned me;
   And Hymen's chains soon bound me to sweet Betsy o' Dundee.

62. BONNIE BROUGHTY FERRY FISHER LASS

1. It was in the month of August one morning by the sea,

When violets and cowslips they so delighted me,

I met a pretty damsel, for an empress she might pass,

And my heart was captivated by that bonnie Broughty Ferry fisher lass.

Chorus:
For the petticoats she wore so short, fell straight below her knee,
Her handsome leg and ankle they quite delighted me;
Her rosy cheeks and yellow hair, none with her could surpass,
With her creel she trudges daily, does my bonnie Broughty Ferry fisher lass.

2. 'Good morning to you, fair maid,' I unto her did say;
   'Why are you up so early, and where go you this way?'
   She said, 'I am going to look for bait, so allow me for to pass,
   For my lines I must get ready,' said the bonnie Broughty Ferry Fisher lass.

3. 'For I must go unto the rocks, the mussels for to pick
   No matter if it rains or snows, the bait I have to get;
   For we all must lend a helping hand, so your pardon I must ask,
   And travel on my journey,' said my bonnie Broughty Ferry fisher lass.

4. For my old father's on the ocean wild, toiling in his boat,
   For to gain an honest livelihood so often he's afloat;
   Whenever he to home returns, he lovingly will clasp
   Unto his aged bosom his hearty fisher lass.'

5. 'When a storm arises on the sea, I'm out upon the pier,
   I'll stand and watch sincerely, for I'm in dread and fear,
   Least he should meet a watery grave, and be snatched from our grasp,
   Then we would wander broken-hearted,' said my bonnie Broughty Ferry
   fisher lass.

20. A Broughty Ferry fisher family.

63. THE ROAD TAE DUNDEE A

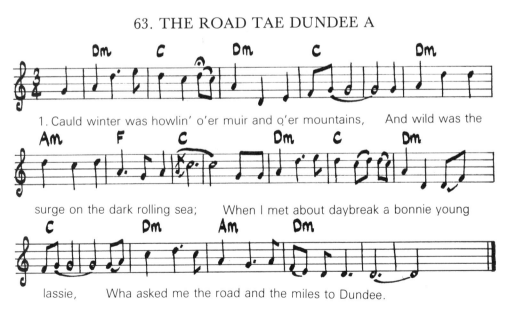

1. Cauld winter was howlin' o'er muir and o'er mountains, And wild was the

surge on the dark rolling sea; When I met about daybreak a bonnie young

lassie, Wha asked me the road and the miles to Dundee.

2. Noo says I, 'Ma wee lassie I cannae weel tell ye,
   The road and the distance I cannae weel gie,
   But if ye'll permit me tae gang a wee bittie,
   I'll show you the road that leads on tae Dundee.'

125

3. Noo the lassie consented and she gied me her airum,
   Ne'er a word did I spier wha the creature might be,
   She appeared like an angel in features an' form,
   As she walked by ma side on the Road tae Dundee.

4. Noo at length wi the hill o' Strathmartine behind us,
   And the spires o' the toon in full view we could see,
   She says, 'Ma kind sir I will never forget ye,
   For showing me sae far on the Road tae Dundee.'

5. 'This ring and this purse take to show I am grateful,
   And some simple token I trust ye'll gie me,
   And in time tae come I'll remember the laddie,
   That showed me the road and the miles tae Dundee.

6. I took a gold pin frae the scarf on ma bosom,
   An' I said, 'Tak ye this in remembrance o' me,'
   And fondly I kissed the sweet lips o' that lassie,
   As I pairted wi' her on the Road tae Dundee.

7. Noo I'll gang intae Vic Torrance an' I'll tak a wee drappie,
   On the road gettin hame it will help me a wee,
   And fondly I'll think on the bonnie wee lassie,
   The lassie I left on the Road tae Dundee.

8. So here's tae that lassie I'll never forget her,
   And every young laddie that's listenin tae me,
   Oh never be sweared tae convoy a wee lassie,
   If it's only tae show her the Road tae Dundee.

As sung by Belle Stewart.
Collected by Maurice Fleming, arranged by Peter Shepheard.

THE ROAD TAE DUNDEE B

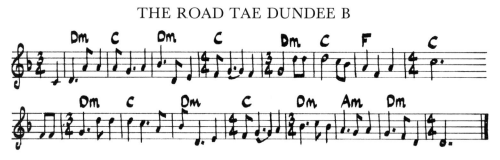

As sung by Charlie Lamb.
Collected by Peter Shepheard.

64. ROSE O' DUNDEE

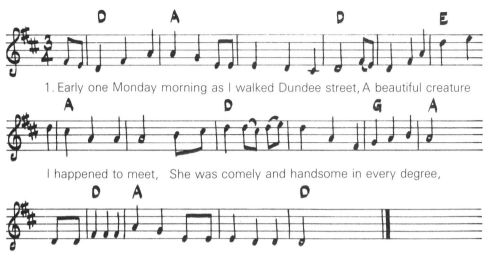

1. Early one Monday morning as I walked Dundee street, A beautiful creature I happened to meet, She was comely and handsome in every degree,

And the title I gave her was the rose o' Dundee.

2. First when I beheld her I could not be sure
   Whether she was an angel or virgin so pure;
   To view her behaviour in every degree,
   You could scarce find her equal in bonnie Dundee.

3. The flame in my bosom so gently did glow,
   To gaze on her beauty I straightway did go;
   Her looks were so loving she enticed me,
   My heart soon belonged to the Rose o' Dundee.

4. I stepped up to her, and thus I did say,
   'Kind nature has formed you my heart to betray;
   And if you'll go with me your guardian I'll be,
   Until we be married in bonnie Dundee.'

5. 'If I should go with you I would do myself wrong,
   For I am engaged with another young man;
   He says he'll be loyal and loving to me –
   He lives in the Hilltown of bonnie Dundee.'

6. 'He is a young sailor brought up in this town,
   He says he will buy me a fine silken gown;
   In the height of the fashion adorned I'll be,
   I'll look like a lady at the kirks o' Dundee.'

7. 'O, foolish young girl, what makes you so vain?
   He prattles with many, but marries with nane;
   He'll leave you a baby to sit on your knee,
   In place of a husband in bonnie Dundee.'

8. Her cheeks blushed like roses, she being a young maid,
   I stepped up to her and lovingly said –
   'Forsake the young sailor and marry with me,
   For ever I'll adore you, the Rose o' Dundee.'

9. 'For all that you've said, sir, it is in vain,
   You may look for some other her favour to gain;
   I ne'er will forsake my young sailor,' said she,
   'For I hope we'll be married in bonnie Dundee.'

10. Now, by this time the young sailor drew nigh,
    And, being well pleased, he made this reply –
    'No other one breathing shall e'er me enjoy,
    But you, my sweet fair one, the Rose o' Dundee.'

11. So now to conclude and finish my song,
    They got buckled together, come right or come wrong,
    Before clerk and clergy they both did agree,
    And now they live happy in bonnie Dundee.

65. MA BONNIE WEE LOCHEE LASS

1. It fell upon a Lammas nicht now I went oot for a stroll, I hadna walked sae very far when I wandered doon by the toll, I'd only gaed one mile or two when a bonnie fair I did pass, 'Twas there I fell in love wi' a bonnie wee Lochee lass.   CHORUS: 'Now whaur are ye gaun, gie me yer han', hoo dae ye dae,' says I, 'Hold up yer head ma bonnie wee lass now dinna be sae shy, Now whaur dae ye bide, whaur dae ye stay, come tell tae me yer name, Will yer father no' be angry now if I was to tak' ye hame?'

2. We sat we cracked a guid lang while aboot a thing or twa,
   We cracked an' cracked until we saw the stars had gaen awa,
   She drew her shawl aroon' her head and quietly she did explain,
   Says she, 'Young man ye'll keep yer word for ye promised tae tak me hame.'

3. An' now we two are married an' happy as we can be,
   She's got two children by her side, anither one on her knee,
   We laugh an' crack at oor fireside an' think o' the times that have passed.
   I'll never forget the nicht I fell in love wi ma Lochee Lass.

As sung by Annie Watkins.
Collected by Maurice Fleming, arranged by Peter Shepheard.

66. AS I CAM OWER STRATHMARTINE MAINS

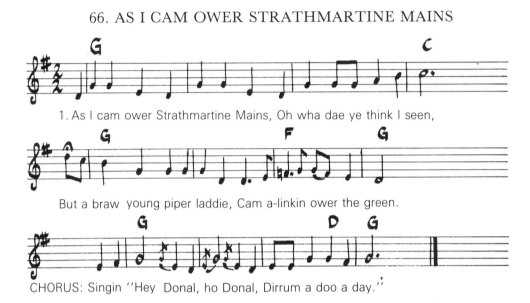

1. As I cam ower Strathmartine Mains, Oh wha dae ye think I seen,

But a braw young piper laddie, Cam a-linkin ower the green.

CHORUS: Singin "Hey Donal, ho Donal, Dirrum a doo a day."

    2. He played a reel an' he played a jig,
       An' he played a sweet strathspey,
       He roosed ma hert till its beat kept time,
       Tae the tappin o' ma tae.

    3. 'Oh I've na gowd tae offer ye,
       For I gaithered little gear,
       But we'll hae love and freedom
       Gin ye'll follow me ma dear.'

    4. 'For there's gowd on the broom o' the Siddelaw Hill,
       Honey fae the heather sweet,
       There's a speckled trout be the hidlin tarn,
       A velvet carpet 'neath yer feet.'

    5. Syne he blew up his chanter,
       An' sic a spring he plays,
       Then I chose love an' freedom,
       Now we wander a' wir days.

Words and music by Mary Brooksbank.
As sung by Mary Brooksbank, recorded by Maurice Fleming.

57. THE BANKS OF SWEET DUNDEE II

A) From Eck Harley, recorded by Peter Shepheard. An unusual version of the tune in that it is in 6/8 rather than the usual 4/4.

B) Jim Reid's tune, arranged by Peter Shepheard.

One of the most famous and widespread of folksongs, this song is also known as 'Undaunted Mary' or 'The Farmer's Daughter'. According to Cecil Sharp, it was '. . . sung by almost every folksinger of the present day'. The number of collected versions seems to confirm this, as there are versions from Berkshire, Somerset, Leeds, North Yorkshire and as far away as the Appalachian mountains and Nova Scotia, let alone the numerous Scottish versions. The story of a farmer's daughter whose uncle bribes the press-gang to steal away her lover had a particular relevance during the nineteenth century. The use of press-gangs to force sailing men into the British navy went on for more than a hundred years, and the press-gang were known to be 'permanently established' in Dundee during 1803. Almost no man with sailor's garb was safe, and the Dundee sailors, usually loud in drunken celebration, kept very quiet during that time.

The literary quality of the song is in no way high, and it has been described by some critics as 'sublime doggerel' (doggerel – trivial, undignified verse). The collector Frank Kidson wrote, 'there is enough tragedy and injured innocence in the ballad to furnish the plot of a penny novelette'. The song was popular as a broadside during the nineteenth century, as so many similar melodramatic ballads were.

58. SCOTS CALLAN O' BONNIE DUNDEE

From the Poets' Box and the singing of Jim Reid.

The air for this song is one of the oldest and most widespread tunes for Scots song, with at least fifteen different songs written to it. It first appears as 'Adew Dundee' in William Dauney's 1838 translation of the Skene Manuscript (c. 1630), where reference is made to the 'ancient' and 'modern' versions. Then it appears in Playford's *Dancing Master* (1688) as 'Bonnie Dundee'. Later, in O'Neill's *Dance Music of Ireland,* it is a jig called 'The Laccarue Boys'.

The first four lines of the song are almost exactly the same as 'Jockey's Escape From Dundee' (No. 28), although 'Scots Callan' is likely to have been the original. Burns added the last verse for inclusion in Johnson's *Musical Museum* (1787-1803).

59. JAMIE FRAE DUNDEE

From a collection printed and sold by J. McFadyen, 'at his Music Ware House, Wilson Street, Glasgow', also called the Watlen Collection, and dated *circa* 1796. It was called there 'The Dundee Lassie', but it turns up as 'Jamie Frae Dundee' in an early nineteenth-century list of broadsides, and again in *The Book of Scottish Song* (1866), edited by Alexander Whitelaw. This sweet, simple love song has rarely appeared in print since.

60. DONALD O' DUNDEE

Written by David Vedder (1790-1854).

Robert Ford, in his *Vagabond Songs and Ballads of Scotland* 1899-1901, wrote: 'Long and still a favourite song in town and country all over the shires of Forfar, Perth and Fife, 'Donald o' Dundee', though frequently printed in chap and other popular collections, has seldom in all its busy career been attributed to its author, David Vedder'. Vedder was born in Orkney and, after having captained a ship on several trips to Greenland, became a tide-surveyor at, among other ports, Dundee. He published many volumes of poetry and collections of other poets' works. Of the tune, Ford wrote that '. . . it goes with a pleasing air, which, I believe, is original'. 'Mess John', in the third verse, is the minister.

61. BETSY O' DUNDEE

Text from a Poets' Box sheet. Tune from the singing of Mr Dorman of New Brunswick, recorded by Helen Creighton for her *Folksongs from Southern New Brunswick*.

That the tune for this song should be lost until it turned up in Canada in the 1960s, with fragments of the song itself, is a remarkable tribute to the strength of oral transmission. Mr Dorman's verses are very similar to the Poets' Box words; compare this verse with verse four:

> Till at length a comely maid, Oh she has my heart betrayed,
> Down by a myrtle shade I espied this lovely she.
> 'Pray tell my lovely fair one your aim and occupation'.
> Quite modestly she answered me, 'I'm Betsy of Dundee'.

62. BONNIE BROUGHTY FERRY FISHER LASS

Text from the Poet's Box. Air is given as 'Shannon Side'.

On the sheet it is claimed that this song was written by J. G. Scott, who ran the Poets' Box from the 1880s till 1906. Whether he was in fact the original author, or merely adapted the lyrics slightly to a local setting is not known, as Gavin Greig collected a song called 'The Bonnie Fisher Lass' which has almost identical words, but omitting the 'Broughty Ferry' in the final line of each verse. The Irish song 'Shannon Side' itself has extremely similar words.

63. THE ROAD TAE DUNDEE

A) From the singing of Belle Stewart, collected by Peter Shepheard.

B) Charlie Lamb's tune, recorded by Peter Shepheard.

This is one of the most widespread of all Dundee love songs. Gavin Greig, John Ord, Ewan MacColl and some Canadian folklorists have all included it in their collections, and there is an Irish version called 'Sweet Carnlough Bay'. Nothing is known of the origin of the song, but the tune is well known and generally referred to as 'the auld way'. The Poets' Box printed a version in which the girl reveals her social standing:

But here's twinty guineas, a Scotch duke my father,
He is bound to support me, I'll make it go free;
Gaung into the Flute Arms and tak a wee drappie,
A body that's trav'ling it helps them a wee.

Gavin Greig thought that the version in which the girl's father is a duke was 'likely to be nearer the original'. Belle Stewart's version also mentions going into a pub, in this case 'Vic Torrance'.

The more familiar tune, called the 'modern' one, is also old and is used with other songs – there is even a parody called 'The Hoor o' Dunblane'.

64. ROSE O' DUNDEE

Text from a Poets' Box sheet. No air given, but the words fit in well with the air of 'Sweet Betsy from Pike', also known as 'Villikins and his Dinah', and the tune to the Scottish song 'The Thrashing Machine'.

65. MA BONNIE WEE LOCHEE LASS

From the singing of Annie Watkins, recorded by Maurice Fleming. Related to 'The Bonnie Wee Tramping Lass'. Possibly a Poets' Box sheet originally.

The song is similar in text and tune to 'The Darvel Dam' known in that part of Scotland – Ayrshire and Lanarkshire. Also related is 'The Bonnie Wee Tramping Lass', and it is possible that this is one of the localised adaptions printed by the Poets' Box. Annie sings her songs with typical Dundee pronunciation: *I* pronounced *Eh'll, I'd* as *Eh'd, whaur* as *whar, gaun* as *gaan,* and so on.

66. AS I CAM OWER STRATHMARTINE MAINS

Recorded from Mary Brooksbank by Maurice Fleming. Mary heard a young tinker diddling this tune, and so was inspired to write the song in celebration of the tinkers' life of freedom. The refrain was possibly borrowed from another song, 'Hey Donald, Howe Donald, Hey Donald Couper!' Mary pronounced Sidlaw as *Siddelaw* in the song.

Humorous Songs

The humorous tradition in Scottish song is well established. Early ballads and songs such as 'The Keech in the Creel' and 'The Auld Man's Mare's Dead' display the very Scottish characteristic of portraying ordinary people in ludicrous situations. 'The Auld Man's Mare's Dead', written by Patie Birnie (1635-c. 1700) of Kinghorn, Fife, describes in great detail everything that is wrong with the 'Auld Man's Mare':

> She had the fiercie and the fleuk,
> The wheezeloch and the wanton yeuk;
> On ilka knee she had a breuk –
> And yet the jad did dee!

> The auld man's mare's dead,
> The puir man's mare's dead,
> The auld man's mare's dead,
> A mile abune Dundee.

During the bothy era, the ability to laugh at misfortunes became a strength. The hardships of life in the bothy were relieved by humour in song, often cruelly directed at unpopular farm owners.

The bothy ballad was to become part of the music hall repertoire, and new songs were written in a 'bothy ballad' style. This type of song remained popular, and during the gramophone record boom, singers such as Willie Kemp and G. S. Morris composed and performed songs like 'McGinty's Meal and Ale' and 'The Buchan Plooman'. Andy Stewart continued this trend into the 1960s when he sang his versions of bothy ballads (one of his 'adapted' songs was 'The Back o' Reres Hill').

For a wider example of songs which celebrate the misfortunes of ordinary folk, we should add to the songs in this section three others, which, though found in other sections, are humorous songs: 'The Beefcan Close', 'Betsy Bell' and 'Indygo Blue'. The attempted robbing of a plooman, in Dundee for the fair, the unfortunate plight of a spinster, the antics of a simple-minded street hawker – although there is an element of cruelty in these subjects, they are very amusing if taken in the right way. By laughing at these ridiculous situations involving people very like those we see every day, we are laughing at our own predicaments and lives, something that the Scots have learned to do rather well.

67. THE IRON HORSE A

1. Come hieland-man, come lowland-man, Come every man on earth, man,
I'll tell ye how I got on atween Dundee and Perth man: I gaed upon an iron
road, a rail they did it ca', man, An' ruggit be an iron horse, an awfu' beast
tae draw, man. CHORUS: Fal – la – la – la – la – la, la – la – la – la – la – la,
Fal – la – la – la – la – la, La – la – la – la – la – la!

2. Noo, first and foremost, next the door
   There stands a wee bit wicket.
   'Twas there they gar'd me pay ma fare,
   An' then shoved me a ticket.
   Then I gaed in an' through the hoose,
   An' sat doon on a kist, man,
   Tae tak a look at a' I saw,
   An' the great big iron beast, man.

3. There were hooses in a lang stracht raw,
   A-stannin upon wheels, man.
   And the chiels wha fed the Iron Horse
   Were as black's a pair o' deils, man.
   But ne'er a thing they gied the beast,
   But fire and coals tae eat, man.
   'Twas the queerest brute that e'er I saw,
   For it had wheels for feet, man.

135

4. Up comes a chap, and roond his cap
    He wore a yellow band, man.
  He telt me for tae tak a seat –
    Said I, 'I'd raither stand, man.'
  He asked me, wis I gaun tae Perth?
    Says I, 'Oh that I be, man;
  But I'm weel eneuch jist whaur I am,
    Because I want tae see, man.'

5. He said I was the queerest chap
    That e'er there was on earth, man,
  For 'twas only the hooses on the wheels
    That gaed 'tween this and Perth, man.
  And then he looked and wondered, tae,
    When he saw I'd nae discernment –
  'Guid sake,' says I, 'I never thocht
    But what the hale concern went.'

6. Noo, the beast it hooched, and aff we gaed,
    Awa through earth and stanes, man.
  It gaed at sic a furious rate,
    I thocht 'twad brak ma banes, man,
  Until at length they ca'd a halt,
    At a place ca'd something Gowrie,
  But deil a thing had I tae dae,
    But jist tae sit and glower aye.

7. Noo, after that they ca'd a halt,
    And in comes yellow band man.
  He asked me for ma ticket,
    An' I a' ma pooches fand, man;
  But ne'er a ticket had I got,
    I'd tint it on the road, man,
  So he made ma pay my fare again,
    Or else go aff tae quod, man.

8. Noo, we're o'er the brig, and 'cross the Tay,
    And landed into Perth, man.
  I think it was the queerest street
    That e're I saw on earth, man;
  For the hooses and the Iron Horse
    Were far abeen the land, man;
  And hoo they got them up the stairs,
    I canna understand, man.

9. Noo, we're o'er the brig, and 'cross the Tay,
   Ma fit upon the sod, man,
And gin tae Dundee I gae back,
   I'll haud anither road, man.
Tho' I should tramp the hale day lang,
   And no be fit to stand, man,
Catch me again when I'm ta'en in
   Wi a chap wi a yellow band, man.

As sung by Eck Harley.
Arranged by Peter Shepheard.

THE IRON HORSE B

Fal   lal di day   fallal didaldididdle fal diddle lay

As sung by Charlie Lamb.
Collected and arranged by Peter Shepheard.

68. THE WIFE O' DUNDEE

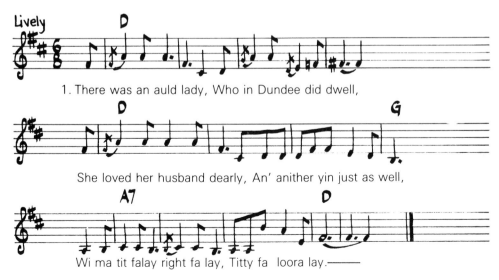

1. There was an auld lady, Who in Dundee did dwell,

She loved her husband dearly, An' anither yin just as well,

Wi ma tit falay right fa lay, Titty fa loora lay.——

2. She gaed tae a doctor,
   Tae see if she could find,
   Some curious sort o' a medical,
   Tae mak her auld man blind.

3. The doctor gie her a marriebone,
   Tae grind it very small,
   An' blow the dust into her husband's eyes,
   Sae he wouldnae see ony at a'.

4. But the doctor wrote a letter,
   An' signed it with his hand,
   An' posted it on tae the auld man,
   So he wid understand.

5. Early next mornin,
   The auld man awoke,
   Sayin, 'Dear auld wife, I'll hae tae droon masel
   For I cannae find ma way.'

6. It's 'Oh dear husband,'
   It's 'Wait tae break o' day,
   An' I'll go steadily wi' ye,
   For I'm fear'd ye lose yer way.'

7. At last they reached the water,
   The water bein' dim
   'Oh dear auld wife, I canna droon masel,
   Ye'll hae tae shove me in.'

8. She staupit forrit, she staupit back
   An' wi an awfu rin,
   The silly auld devil he stood aside,
   An' she gaed headlang in.

9. Oh splashin, dashin, like a juck,
   'Oh help me,' she did roar.
   Oh wisnae she a silly auld wife,
   She couldna soom ashore.

10. But there came a kind hearted gentleman,
    Who couldna see her droon,
    An' wi the end o' his walkin' stick,
    He shoved her the further doon,
        Wi ma tit fa lay right fa lay,
        Titty fa loora lay.

As sung by Eck Harley, Cupar.
Collected and arranged by Peter Shepheard.

69. THE PEAR TREE

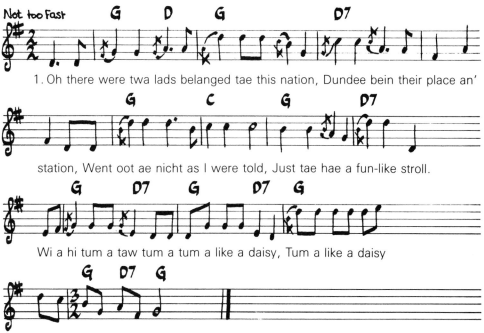

1. Oh there were twa lads belanged tae this nation, Dundee bein their place an'
station, Went oot ae nicht as I were told, Just tae hae a fun-like stroll.

Wi a hi tum a taw tum a tum a like a daisy, Tum a like a daisy

wi a tum a lum a lay.

2. For noo on the road they spied a pear tree,
   There grew pears as fine as could be,
   So for a pear they were inclined,
   So up the pear tree they did climb.

3. For up the pear tree they were landed,
   Up the pear tree they were stranded,
   It wisna the pears that taen ma ee,
   'Twas the lad an' the lass lyin in alow the tree.

4. So this young man he began tae unlace her,
   This young man began tae embrace her,
   Ta'en aff his coat tae save her goun,
   When a' the pears cam a-rummlin' doon.

5. So this young man he looked up in wonder,
   As we battered doon the pears like thunder,
   So up he got an' awa did flee,
   Leavin his coat lyin in alow the tree.

6. So the owner of the coat we did enquire,
   The owner of the coat wis our desire,
   The owner of the coat we never found out,
   So we had a damn guid coat for nowt.

139

7. Noo a' ye lads whaur e'er ye may be,
   Dinna ging coortin' alow a pear tree,
   For if he do ye'll spoil the fun,
   When a' the pears cam a-rummlin' doon.
         Wi a hi tum a taw tum a tum a like a daisy,
         Tum a like a daisy wi a tum a lum a lay.

As sung by Dave Marshall, Methven.
Collected and arranged by Peter Shepheard.

70. I'LL AWA HAME

1. Noo. I'll no bide wi ma granny nae mair, I'll no bide wi ma granny

nae mair, She skelps ma face an' she pu's ma hair, An' I'll no bide

wi ma granny nae mair.

2. I'll awa hame tae ma mother I will,
   I'll awa hame tae ma mother I will,
   She keeps a wee shop at the tap o' the hill,
   An' she sells a wee drappie at sixpence a gill.

3. Now here is a chorus I'll sing it tae you,
   If you like tae join it that's what you can do,
   So here comes the words an' we'll all go along,
   We'll put out the music the rhythm an' song.

4. 'Cos I'll no bide wi ma granny nae mair,
   I'll no bide wi ma granny nae mair,
   She skelps ma face an' she pu's a' ma hair,
   Now I'll no bide wi ma granny nae mair.

As sung by Annie Watkins.
Collected by Maurice Fleming, arranged by Peter Shepheard.

140

71. DUNDEE JAIL

1. 'Oh, have you seen my Mary Ann?' was one time all the go;
But now 'tis neither pot nor pan — 'tis 'Dundee Jail You Know'.

CHORUS: Oh, may there ne'er to this poor house a son of Adam go;
For puss can't live, nor e'en a mouse, in Dundee Jail you know.

2. A warder, with majestic form, soon shows you where to go;
His voice to rules makes you conform in Dundee Jail you know.

3. A suit ye get, without your aid, makes you a frightfu beau;
They put gay fashion in the shade in Dundee Jail you know.

4. The doctor calls to make you whole, the parson comes to sow
The Word into your darkened soul, in Dundee Jail you know.

5. No whisky here, no bitter beer, nor smoking now you know,
And not a thing which tends to cheer in Dundee Jail you know.

6. Each day you get three scanty meals in sunshine rain or snow;
The drunkard's sad complaint soon heals in Dundee Jail you know.

7. The vile plank bed could tell a tale of agony and woe;
Groans, sighs, and tears – of no avail – in Dundee Jail you know.

8. A prisoner's life is a dreary one; no knocking to and fro;
And sad to think all sport is done in Dundee Jail you know.

9. There's not a thing in life we hear but when the cock does crow;
It minds of liberty – so near to Dundee Jail you know.

10. The cruel and tyrant husband gets tanned on diet low;
And vows no more to lift his hand – in Dundee Jail you know.

141

11. The poacher too has lost his fame since he came in our row;
    But he must now give up his game in Dundee Jail you know.

12. I'm free, but when I bring to mind, my eyes with salt tears flow,
    To think of those I left behind in Dundee Jail you know.

13. Take this advice before we part, be ye a friend or foe –
    Do what is right where'er thou art, lest Dundee Jail you know.

72. SANDY'S MILL

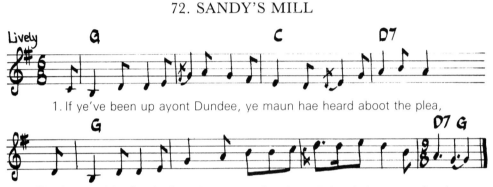

1. If ye've been up ayont Dundee, ye maun hae heard aboot the plea,

That's raised by Sandy Grant's trustees For the mill that belangs tae Sandy.

2. For Sandy he belangs the mill,
   Sandy he belangs the mill,
   Sandy he belangs the mill,
   And the mill belangs tae Sandy.

3. Said the man tae Sandy, lend me your mill,
   And Sandy says, I'll lend you my mill,
   And the man got a len o' Sandy's mill,
   But the mill belangs tae Sandy.

4. Sandy lent the man his mill,
   But the mill belangs tae Sandy still,
   Sandy lent the man his mill,
   But the mill belang'd tae Sandy.

5. A' sense o' sin and shame is gone,
   A' love atween the two has gone,
   They're claiming noo a lien on,
   The mill that belang'd tae Sandy.

6. Sandy he belangs the mill,
   Sandy he balangs the mill,
   Sandy he belangs the mill,
   And the mill belangs tae Sandy.

As sung by Archie Webster.
Collected and arranged by Peter Shepheard.

142

73. THE BOMBIN RAID

1. Hey listen and I'll tell ye hoo the Jocks spent their New Year, Standin in the b-loomin trench wi the mud right up to here, All sodden through, aye through and through. Now Mister Kaiser said ''Ha ha the Jocks are fu the noo, So we'll go over wi the best o' luck an' see what we can do.'' So a scheme was laid   for a bombin raid. CHORUS: Noo they're sorry that they made that bombin raid, They were up agin the Men o' Marmalade,   For if Fritz had only known in that trench was Dundee's Own, He would never never made that bombin raid.

2. Now they opened with artillery, terrific rapid fire,
   Should auld acquaintance be forgot, the shells fell on oor wire,
      The cunning chap, to make a gap.
   But the Jocks they lay in wait, in their hearts they knew no fear,
   When Mr Fritz comes in oor trench we'll let him know we're here,
      We're Scotsmen through, aye through an' through.

3. Now when those German plans went wrang they didn't know what to do,
   'Gotten Himmel', they all cried, 'The Jocks are standing to.'
      They rubbed their eyes, they were surprised.
   For when they reached our old barbed wire our rifles they did roar,.
   Alas, alas poor 'Ally Men', you've knocked at the wrang door,
      Nae welcome here this guid New Year.

Words and music by Tom Shannon, Lochee.
As sung by Charlie Lamb, Lochee.
Arranged by Peter Shepheard.

74. ROBBIE AN' GRANNY

1. Noo Robbie and Granny they went tae the toon, An' atween themselves twa
they did spend half a croon, For ilka drink Robbie drank Granny drank two,
And in a crack the auld buddy got fu.
Fal diddle lal, fal diddle lay, Fal diddle lal lal, fal diddle lay.

2. Noo Robbie an' Granny they were comin hame,
   When the buddy's fit slippit an' Granny fell in,
   It's, 'Noo Robbie, noo Robbie, noo Robbie noo,
   I hae fa'n in a ditch ye maun gie me a pu'.'

144

3. Noo Robbie pu'd at her until he fell back,
   Wi an awfie like rushle an' near broke his back;
   He cursed an' he ca'd her a drucken auld soo,
   But aye the puir buddy cried, 'Pu', Robbie pu'.'

4. Noo, Robbie pu'd at her until he wis sair,
   Says Robbie tae Granny, 'I'll pu' ye nae mair,'
   She hirstled, she struisled, she got up again,
   An' wi the help o' pair Robbie the buddy won hame.

5. Noo Robbie an' Granny sat in the neuk end,
   Say's Granny tae Robbie, 'As ye may depend,
   The claes that I hae intended for you,
   I'll sell for siller seen ye wouldnae pu'.'

6. Say's Robbie tae Granny, 'Can this be the end,
   I'll tak a wife as yet may depend;
   And if ever she happens for tae get fu,
   An' fa's in a ditch I'll gie her a pu'.'
       Fal diddle lal, fal diddle lay,
       Fal diddle lal lal, fal diddle lay.

As sung by Charlie Lamb, Lochee.
Collected by Maurice Fleming. Arranged by Peter Shepheard.

75. ANDRA CARNEGIE

1. Said Andra Carnegie to me ae day, I've got tired of my money for aince in a
way; We'll gang to yon toon on the banks of the Tay, And we'll pent it red
with a "Hip Hoo Ray!", For I've made up my mind to gang on the spree, And
we'll gang to yon toon they ca "Bonny Dundee"; There's naebody kens me
there ava, An' we'll gang on the loose for a month or twa.

CHORUS: Wi a million a money an' a' an' a', Wi a million a money an' a' an' a',

Andra Car-negie an me gaed awa, awa, Wi a million a money an' a' an' a'.

2. For a start we drank the Bodega dry,
   An' we Yam Bucked the Buffet forby, forby,
   An' we drank oot the Perthshire o' every drap,
   Then up to the 'Caffie' we took a stap.
   An' after we'd finished that flowing bowl
   We 'Pletted' alang to the Metrapol,
   Then at 9 p.m. we got baith flung oot
   Wi' a gentle help frae the waiter's boot.

Chorus:
Wi a million a money an' a' an' a',
Wid ever we get rid o't ava, ava,
Says Andra Carnegie ge'wa, ge'wa,
We'll be doon to a maik in a week or twa.

3. Says Andra Carnegie to me, old pal,
   We'll do a night in the Queen's Hotel,
   There we'll sit an' we'll booze for an oor or twa,
   Aye, an' we'll sleep thegither an' a' an' a',
   So hires a taxi an' awa we go
   The maitter o' twa hundred yairds or so,
   And to show the driver his hert was guid,
   We signed him a cheque for a thousand quid.

Chorus:
Wi a million a money an' a' an' a',
Wi a million a money an' a' an' a',
The weeks they slippit awa, awa,
And the million a money an' a' an' a'.

4. Now the outcome o' oor big caroose,
   We drank the Toon o' Dundee oot o' booze,
   And Neddie Scrymgeour stood aghast,
   For prohibition had come at last,
   We'd had the D.T.s for the fourteenth time,
   Then Andra found oot that he hidna a dime,
   Then I awoke wi an afa scream,
   And found it was only a dream, a dream.

Chorus:
Wi a million a money an' a' an' a',
Wi a million a money an' a' an' a',
Andra Carnegie he fadit awa, awa,
And his million a money an' a' an' a'.

Collected by Maurice Fleming.

76. THE NICHT THAT OOR MAG HAD HER BAIRN

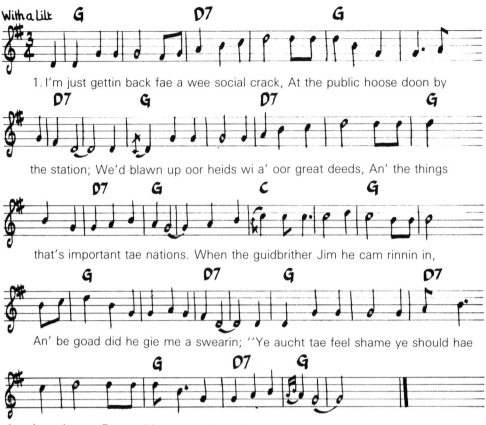

1. I'm just gettin back fae a wee social crack, At the public hoose doon by the station; We'd blawn up oor heids wi a' oor great deeds, An' the things that's important tae nations. When the guidbrither Jim he cam rinnin in, An' be goad did he gie me a swearin; "Ye aucht tae feel shame ye should hae been hame, For yer Maggie she's hae'in her bairn.——

2. Noo I didna tak time tae bid them guid nicht,
   But oot the back door I gaed spinnin;
   I ran up the lane, the nearest road hame,
   Never lookin tae see whaur I'm runnin.
   When I fell ower a stone, nearly broke ma shin bane,
   An' rowed intae a heap o' coo sharin;
   Ma claes were a sicht, 'twad gie ye a fricht,
   The nicht that oor Mag had her bairn.

3. Oh when I got tae the door there wis whisky galore,
   On the table wis cheese, the best goudie;
   When a neebour I spied an' here's what she cried,
   'Ye'd best run awa for the houdie.'
   Wi a glass in her hand she bid me no stand,
   'Run awa noo for Mistress McLaren;
   She's the best in the toon when a woman lies doon,
   An' ye'll soon see a bonnie braw bairn.'

148

4. Noo I ran for the midwife an' I soon fund her oot,
   She thocht I wis oot o' ma senses;
   For I rolled on the floor an' started tae roar,
   'Hurry up wife an' I'll pay a' expenses.
   If ye come tae ma wife or she'll soon lose her life
   She's as fat as five bundles o' yairn,
   If ye make her wame richt ye'll be weel pay'd the nicht,
   The nicht that oor Mag had her bairn.'

As sung by Charlie Lamb, Lochee.
Collected by Maurice Fleming. Arranged by Peter Shepheard.

67. THE IRON HORSE

A) Tune from Archie Webster, text as sung by Eck Harley from his copy of the Poets' Box sheet, bought after hearing the song sung by Will Antoun at Bagersie in the 1930s. The tune is a version of 'Smith's a Gallant Fireman', a well-known strathspey. The chorus was not sung by Archie or Eck but is included here as given in Ford's *Vagabond Songs and Ballads* (1899-1901).

There have been a few collected versions of this song, all remarkably similar. Ford's was the earliest, but it was still being sung this century, and according to him it was written by Charles Balfour, a stationmaster at Glencarse on the Dundee-Perth line. Balfour first sang it at a 'festival of railway servants' in 1848, and he maintained that the story of the yokel who believed that the whole of Dundee station would be transported to Perth was based on a true incident.

Ewan MacColl noted a version at Dundee loco shed, and according to A. L. Lloyd, '. . . it remained popular in the neighbourhood of Perth and Dundee for many years, and was a favourite in the ploughman's bothies of Aberdeenshire'. The tune that MacColl uses is a set of 'The Piper o' Dundee', but the more usual tune is 'Smith's a Gallant'.

B) Charlie Lamb's tune, collected from him by Peter Shepheard. Charlie Lamb claims that his grandfather, who was a guard on the railways, worked on the same train as the composer, whom he said was the driver.

68. THE WIFE O' DUNDEE

From Eck Harley, recorded by Peter Shepheard. Eck heard this song at the harvest home at Rhynd Farm, by Leuchars in Fife, in 1921, when he was thirteen years old. It was sung by Jimmy Kiddie, a bothy lad from the nearby Pusk Farm. The song was a great favourite among the women workers at the Rhynd at that time. Eck's version has been recorded by Cilla Fisher and Artie Trezise on Topic 12TS405.

69. THE PEAR TREE

From the singing of Dave Marshall of Methven. Peter Shepheard recorded this version of 'The Pear Tree' for publication in the programme/song book of the 1968 Blairgowrie Festival, at which Dave was a guest. When The Blairgowrie Festival started in 1966 it was the first festival organised by the Traditional Music and Song Association of Scotland (TMSA). Dave (aged thirty-six at the time) had learned the song twenty years earlier from a lad who stayed on the bothy at Westhaven.

70. I'LL AWA HAME

From the singing of Annie Watkins, recorded by Maurice Fleming.

Other versions of this song give slightly different words: 'She skelps ma bum an' she pu's ma hair' instead of 'face'. Annie Watkins pronounces the words of the song in typical Dundee fashion – 'I'll' pronounced 'Eh'll', and 'will', 'hill' and 'gill' pronounced 'wull', 'hull' and 'jull'. The hill in question is of course the Hilltown.

71. DUNDEE JAIL

From the Poets' Box. Air given is 'John Anderson My Jo'.

72. SANDY'S MILL

As sung in part by Archie Webster, Strathkinness, collected by Peter Shepheard. Archie remembers this song as he heard it when he was about five years old from Jockie Colville at Sinacus Castle, Balmullo. Verses 3 and 5 are from The Rymour Club, Edinburgh's *Miscellanea,* Vol. 1 (1906-11). At one time, simple rhymes were used to illustrate various local procedures. These rhymes were collected and presented in a book by George Outram called *Legal and Other Lyrics.* 'Sandy's Mill', one of these legal lyrics, was intended to explain the law of *lien,* that is, the right to keep someone else's property until a debt due on it has been paid. From these academic beginnings, the song became used as a nonsense 'mouth music' song for dancing, and has been recorded from Isabel Sutherland to the tune 'The Rakes of Mallow'.

73. THE BOMBIN RAID

Words and Music by Tom Shannon, Lochee. As sung by Charlie Lamb.

The 'Ally men' were the Germans, after the French *Allemagne* meaning Germany. Dundee's Own were the 4th/5th Black Watch, the Dundee batallion of the Black Watch based in Perth, called 'the men o' marmalade'.

74. ROBBIE AN' GRANNY

As sung by Charlie Lamb of Lochee, collected by Maurice Fleming. Jim Reid also has a version of this song, learned ten years ago from Mrs Falconer of Dundonald Street, Dundee. She was then in her 'seventies and she in turn had the song from her mother. A few verses are in Greig's *Folk Song of the North East.*

75. ANDRA CARNEGIE

Collected by Maurice Fleming. Sung to 'Wi' a Hundred Pipers'. This song of a gargantuan pub crawl in Dundee mentions some of the old Dundee pubs. Another song about the old pubs went like this:

> Monday nicht's the Dundee Arms,
> Tuesday nicht's the Pump,
> Wednesday nicht's the Arctic Bar.
> Where maybe we'll get drunk.

> Thursday nicht's the Hood and Scott,
> Friday nicht's the Star,
> And we finish on a Setterday nicht
> In the Old Bank Bar.

76. THE NICHT THAT OOR MAG HAD HER BAIRN

As sung by Charlie Lamb, recorded by Maurice Fleming.

Charlie Lamb learned this song from another Lochee man, Willie Sime, a local builder, when they were both members of the Lochee Burns Club. It crops up in another Dundee song. 'The Bureau' (No. 45): 'I sang that sang ''Oor Maggie Had a Bairn''/But the gaffer didna like that sang, / The job didna rin for verra lang, Cann'ries, bye bye!'

Dundee has seen many changes in her long history, but the past twenty years must have seen the most drastic changes of all. The incidence of large supermarkets, shopping centres and office blocks, along with the areas of waste ground in the city, commemorate what writer David Phillips calls 'The Great Knockin' Doon' – the clearance of the 'sixties.

Mention to young Dundonians the Overgate, the Wellgate, the Hawkhill and Lochee, and they are likely to picture modern shopping centres and University buildings. Yet these areas were once thriving communities, and streets which were alive with bustling activity. The Wellgate was an interesting place, not locked up at night as the new concrete and glass shopping centre is now. The Hawkhill was a well populated street with old shops and grand pubs; now it has been cleared for a new bypass, and the shop, the pubs and the people have gone. Yet, looking at the old photographs of Dundee, many people catch the magic of the streets, the wynds, the pubs and the shops, and wonder whatever happened to the town. A good number of older people still cannot understand why certain things had to go: the West Station, the Town House ('the Pillars'), Lochee. However, one can only lament the passing of the old places, because whether they were communities alive with social activity or, as some people see it, overcrowded slums, they are gone forever.

Two songs by local songwriters neatly express the sentiments of many Dundonians.

21. A familiar sight in Dundee today, where whole areas are made up of derelict mills and factories.

77. CATHERINE STREET

1. Ae day I wandered a' alane, Ma thochts contrived tae mak me greet,

It wis on a wee bit skelp o grund, That aince wis kent as Catherine Street.

2. The demolition squad's been there,
   An' every stick an' stane they cleared,
   They said the hooses were nae fit,
   For modern faimilies tae be reared.

3. I suppose I must agree wi them,
   The conveniences I'm sure were bad,
   But the fowk in thae auld days lang syne,
   Fair made the maist o' what they had.

4. And as I lingered there a while,
   Ma sadness slowly turned tae joy,
   When mindin on the pals I had,
   An' the games we played when just a boy.

5. At pinner an' pig an' kick the can,
   At closie heiders an' a' the rest,
   Or at the fitba in the street,
   The Craithie lads could beat the best.

6. Then we'd slip in tae Mrs Pike's,
   That's if we'd money tae oor name,
   An' a penny vantis we wad buy,
   Tae refresh us for another game.

7. In the march o' time a' things must change,
   A' for the best, or so they say,
   But sometimes I think it wad be braw,
   If the clocks could go back for just a day.

Words and music by Jim Reid.
By permission of Springthyme Music.

78. PULL DOON THE CHIMNEYS

Sung to the tune of 'The Bonnets of Bonnie Dundee' (No. 10).

1. If ye live in the Whitfield hoosin' estate,
   If ye live in Mid Craigie or doon the Seagate,
   If ye gang up the Hilltoon or up tae Lochee,
   Ye'll ken it's no' bonnie in Bonnie Dundee.

   Chorus:
   Come pull doon the chimneys and close a' the mills,
   Demolish the fact'ries where'er ye will,
   Remove the West Port and soon ye will see,
   There's naethin' at a' left o' Bonnie Dundee.

2. If you walk up the Hawkhill and doon the Blackness,
   You'll find that the hooses are a' in a mess,
   You'll be lucky tae find ane that's nae fa'in doon,
   In fact that's the story a' ower the toon.

3. Come pull doon the tenements and leave a big space,
   It's happening aroond ye a' ower the place;
   They'll pull ye doon tae if ye stand long enough,
   An' grass ye a' ower wi landscapin turf!

Words and music by Catherine Smith.
As sung by Catherine Smith.

79. COMIN OWER THE TAY BRIG

CHORUS: Comin ower the Tay Brig tae bonnie Dundee, Oh the braes of Balgay

and Law Hill grand tae see, Oh ma hert it's sae full, there's a tear in ma ee,

Comin ower the Tay brig tae bonnie Dundee.

1. Oh the world is sae wide, I have travelled sae far,
   Daein ma duty in peace or in war,
   But there's aye a sweet longing that comes over me,
   Tae be ower the Tay brig in bonnie Dundee.

2. Now for sweet foreign beauties my comrades would sigh,
   An' although I had seen them I just passed them by;
   But I'll hope that wee lassie's still waiting for me,
   As I speed ower the Tay brig tae bonnie Dundee.

3. Oh lassies an' laddies ye wander frae hame,
   Ye search the wide world seekin riches or fame,
   Here's a wish that I'll gie that ye'll soon be like me,
   Comin ower the Tay brig tae bonnie Dundee.

   Chorus:
   Comin ower the Tay brig tae bonnie Dundee,
   Oh the braes o' Balgay and Law Hill grand tae see,
   Oh ma hert it's sae full, there's a tear in mae ee,
   Comin over the Tay brig tae bonnie Dundee.

Words and music by Stuartie Foy.

155

80. WE'RE NO AWA TAE BIDE AWA

1. As I was walking doon the Overgate, I met wi' Johnnie Scobie.

I says, 'Man, will ye hae a hauf?' He says, 'Man, that's ma hoabbie!'

Chorus:
For we're no' awa tae bide awa,
For we're no' awa tae leave ye;
We're no' awa tae bide awa,
We'll aye come back an' see ye.

2. Oh, we had a hauf, and anither hauf,
And then we had anither,
And she got drunk, and he got drunk,
And we a' went hame thegither!

As sung by Catherine Smith, Lochee.

156

77. CATHERINE STREET

Written by Jim Reid, about a street in which he was brought up. Jim can be heard singing this song on the first Foundry Bar Band L.P. on Springthyme SPR1007. Reprinted with permission from Springthyme Music.

78. PULL DOON THE CHIMNEYS

Written by Catherine Smith of Lochee.

Although during the past two or three years efforts have been made in Dundee to conserve and redevelop old buildings, this has come too late for many areas in the city.

79. COMIN OWER THE TAY BRIG

Words and music by Stuartie Foy, Dundee, recorded from him by Peter Shepheard.

At the start of the last war when Stuartie's son was leaving Dundee to join the navy, he took the train south over the Tay Bridge. Stuartie composed this song, and it has become one of his most popular songs ever since.

80. WE'RE NO AWA TAE BIDE AWA

From the singing of Catherine Smith.

A very popular song in Dundee and in Scotland generally. It is not clear whether there were local variants in each town, or whether the 'Overgate' version is in fact the original.

Appendix. Notes on Singers

Mary Brooksbank

Any study of folksong in Dundee would be incomplete without mention of Mary Brooksbank, whose songs, especially the famous 'Jute Mill Song', are widely known and sung. Born Mary Soutar in Aberdeen 'on a raw-cold winter's day, 15th December 1897', Mary was blind for the first twelve months of her life. Her father, a dock labourer, and her mother, a fisher lass, moved to Dundee when Mary was eight, to the foot of the Overgate in the Pump Close. Later the family lived in overcrowded conditions at Blackness Road, and then Blackscroft.

After her eleventh birthday, Mary received very little formal education, as she was frequently off school to look after the younger members of the family while her mother worked in the jute mill. Her father was often out of work, and frequently away from home looking for jobs. Mary began work in the mill as a shifter at the age of thirteen, eventually becoming a spinner.

Maurice Fleming met Mary in 1964, when he started recording her songs and reminiscences, and since then she has also been recorded by the School of Scottish Studies at the University of Edinburgh. Singing came easily to Mary, as the Brooksbanks were a singing family. Most of the neighbouring families sang too, and there was always music-making going on. It was while Mary was nursing her sick mother that she began writing poetry and songs, which she eventually published in 1966, in a collection called *Sidlaw Breezes*. The cost of the book was covered by Mary herself, and she lost money on it. It has been reprinted since her death by David Winter and Son Ltd., at the instigation of Dundee writer David Phillips.

During the folkclub days of the 1960s, Mary was always delighted to sing in the clubs and pass on her songs to younger folksingers. Her folk poetry is of high merit, while her songs, whether entirely original or based on snatches of traditional songs, are filled with vitality. Her songs of the mill and the hardships of the jute workforce are from first-hand experience, and invaluable in telling the story of the demise of the industry. Mary died in 1980, aged eighty-two (Songs 19, 21, 32, 37, 38, 42, 43, 44, 66).

Stewart Brown

Stewart Brown was born in Dundee in 1936 where he works in publishing. In 1965 he formed *The Lowland Folk Four* together with his wife Anne, his brother Ramsay and a friend Phil Gore. The group became widely known on radio and TV and made a record 'Eh'll tell the Boaby' that included many Dundee songs. Stewart has taken an interest in collecting local songs and has written several himself. The group recently reformed as *Lowland Folk* and produced a show at the Dundee Rep entitled *Oh Bonnie Dundee*. They have also made a new record *Time to be Singing Again* on Balaena Records (Songs 25, 30, 53).

Alex Clarke
Alex Clarke, now aged 48, belongs to Dundee where he is a butcher. He started on stage as a singer when he was a boy, and over the years he has taken part in several concert parties. His powerful singing was first recorded by Maurice Fleming in 1968 (Song 45a).

Maurice Fleming
Maurice Fleming is a journalist in Dundee. A native of Blairgowrie, he did voluntary fieldwork for the School of Scottish Studies in its early years. His first notable coup was his recordings of the Stewarts of Blair in 1953. He made numerous recordings of travelling people as well as other singers in Dundee, including Mary Brooksbank whom he was responsible for bringing to the School's attention. He was a founder member of Dundee Folksong Club and the TMSA.

Stuartie Foy
Dundee born and bred, *Stuartie Foy* is now aged 93 and recently celebrated his 70th wedding anniversary. He has always enjoyed entertaining, and his father was a well-known stage entertainer before him, specialising in a comic act dressed as a woman. Stuartie, who learned some of his songs from his father, started out at church socials, joined a band as drummer and was soon in regular demand as a singer and entertainer. In the '20s and '30s he played all the big halls in Scotland including the Usher Hall in Edinburgh. He had several offers to go full-time, but he always kept on his job in the jute mills where he rose to become foreman. David Phillips the Dundee journalist has recorded some of his repertoire of songs and recitations for the Dundee museum, and new recordings for the book were made by Peter Shepheard in 1985 (Songs 34c, 79).

Eck Harley
Eck Harley was born at Lucklaw farm, Leuchars in Fife in 1908. He fee'd at Logie at 14 years of age and drove his first pair of horse at Kinninmonth near Ceres, later working as a shepherd on farms in Fife and Angus. He learned some of his songs from his mother, some from other farm workers, and others from song sheets he bought at the Poet's Box in Dundee's Overgate. He and his wife now live in Cupar where he was first recorded by Peter Shepheard in 1968. Through his singing some fine old songs have become widely known, and some have been recorded by Artie Trezise and Cilla Fisher on their albums. He has been a guest at Kinross Festival and latterly at Auchtermuchty Festival where he won the local singer cup in 1981 (Songs 33a, 34a, 35a, 57a, 68).

Charlie Lamb

Charlie Lamb was born in 1927 and brought up in Lochee where he still lives, in a family with a strong tradition of singing and music making. Every Friday night the family gathered round the fire and his father used to sing, tell stories and recite – a tradition carried on from his father before him. Charlie and his father Fred Lamb were founder members in the late 1940s of the revived Lochee Burns Club which still has a weekly 'Scottish and Burns Night'. In the early 1950s Charlie, his brother Fred and brother-in-law Charlie Smith got together a group *The Thistle Three* to sing at local concerts accompanying themselves with mouth organ and mandolin. It was a tape recording of this group that Charlie passed to Maurice Fleming in 1972. Charlie was recorded again for the book by Peter Shepheard in 1985 (Songs 55, 63b, 67b, 73, 74, 76).

Dave Marshall

Dave Marshall was born in 1931 at Panlathy farm near Carnoustie where his father was fee'd as a horseman. After he left school he worked on the farms around Dundee and Perth, first as a horseman and later as a tractorman, and he is now a tractorman with Dundee Parks Department. In 1968 he was recorded by Peter Shepheard and invited as a guest to the Blairgowrie Festival. He was a regular contestant at the annual diddling competitions, particularly at Kettins near Coupar Angus, the last of which was held around 1980. Until they recently disbanded he was a member of *The Fife Yokels* bothy group with whom he made three L.P.s. He is not only a fine diddler and bothy singer but also plays melodeon and mouth organ (Song 69).

Jim Reid

Jim Reid who belongs to Dundee and now lives in Letham, Angus has developed a reputation as one of Scotland's finest singers. A founder member of Arbroath's famous *Foundry Bar Band,* Jim sings and plays with them on their records and has recently recorded his own solo album on Springthyme Records. He was a member of the Dundee Folk Club in the 1960s and sang then with a local folk group *The Shifters* and later with *The Taysiders.* He has made a special study of the songs and poetry of Dundee and Angus, composing some songs himself and setting to music the poetry of Violet Jacob and Helen Cruickshank. He has been recorded for the *Oddysey* and *Music Makars* series on Radio Scotland. Over the years he has been an enthusiastic member of the TMSA, of which he is a past chairman, and he helped found the now famous traditional music festival at Keith (Songs 5, 6, 27, 31b, 35b, 39, 54, 56, 57b, 58, 77).

Peter Shepheard

A singer and folksong collector, *Peter Shepheard* was a founder member of St. Andrews Folk Club in 1962. During the 1960s he collected songs in Ireland, England and Scotland and developed a particular interest in the songs of Fife and Dundee. He recorded a rich harvest of songs among the travelling folk gathered in Blairgowire for the berry picking and, in 1966, he helped start the Blairgowrie Festival from which grew the TMSA of which he is a past chairman. In the early '70s he worked in Fisheries Biology in Canada where he also continued his folksong interests collecting songs in New Brunswick and Newfoundland. He now lives near Kingskettle in Fife and runs the record company Springthyme Records which specialises in songs and music from Scotland's folk tradition.

Belle Stewart

Belle Stewart was born in 1906 in a traveller's tent at Claypotts farm on the banks of the Tay at Caputh near Dunkeld where her father was engaged in pearl fishing on the river. Belle learned her songs within the family circle from her father and brothers and from other travellers. Belle and her late husband Alex owned a berryfield at Alyth in the 1950s. Together with their children Sheila and Cathy they became well known in the 1960s as *The Stewarts of Blair,* making several records for Topic Records. The family were first discovered in 1953 by Maurice Fleming who passed on his recordings to Hamish Henderson in the School of Scottish Studies in Edinburgh. Belle and her two daughters have recently made a new album for Lismor. The family have played at folk clubs, festivals and concerts throughout the British Isles and have had several tours overseas (Songs 31a, 63a).

Annie Watkins

Annie Watkins was born and brought up in Dundee and now lives in sheltered housing in the Dens Park area. For many years she has entertained at church socials and old folk's clubs. She has an interesting repertoire of Dundee songs, she is never stuck for a song to sing and has composed several herself. She was first recorded by Maurice Fleming in 1968 (Songs 32, 41, 45b, 65, 70).

Archie Webster

Archie Webster was born in 1918 at Pusk farm near Leuchars where his father was on the fourth pair of horses. Archie was given his first pair at the age of 13 at Thornbank near Blebocraigs in Fife, and he spent many years as a horseman. Archie has an enormous repertoire of old balladry which he learned from his mother and her brothers and from his paternal grandparents as well as from other farm workers. However, it is not as a singer that he is best known but as a Burns reciter. He has composed a number of songs and poems mostly in Scots, and several of his songs have achieved wider currency through the folksong revival, particularly his own composition 'The Last of the Clydesdales'. Peter Shepheard started collecting his repertoire in 1968 (Songs 67, 72). We are sorry to say that since we went to press, Archie died on 6th August, 1985.

Glossary

1. THE CONSTABLE OF DUNDEE
   ae – one; fey – mad; goud – gold; browst – brew

2. BROUGHTY WA'S
   wat – wet; burd – girl

3. BONNIE ANNIE LIVIESTON
   Erse – Gaelic; gin – if; shoon – shoes (horseshoes); kin – family;
   ha' – hall; brae – hill; muckle – much; taen – one; aboon – above

4. THERE CAM A LADDIE FRAE THE NORTH
   saut – salt; haud – hold; muckle – much; abeen – above

6. THE SKIPPER O' DUNDEE
   wons – stays; wistna – knew not; bleeze – blaze; steer – bother/row;
   kent – known; sicht – sight; warsled – wrestled; wecht – weight;
   pow – head

8. THE ROON-MOO'ED SPADE
   spaiks – the spokes used to carry the coffin; skirl – shreik;
   hairy – heavy; sonsie quine – well-built woman; maun – must;
   tak tent – take heed; fat – what; steer – disturb; pock – sack;
   Glenarf – brand of whisky

9. THE WIFE O' DENSIDE
   howdie – midwife; Jeffrey – the Wife's lawyer;
   tippet – a length of twisted hair, also a hangman's halter

10. THE BONNETS OF BONNIE DUNDEE
    Duinewassals – Highlanders

11. KILLIECRANKIE
    braw – neat; brankie – finely dressed; cantie – cheerful;
    clankie – a shot, hit; gart – made; ayont – beyond; loof – palm;
    sour slaes – awful killing

12. LADY DUNDEE'S LAMENT
    mools – the soil of a grave

13. THE PIPER O' DUNDEE
    spring – tune; brent new – brand new; fou – drunk;
    their lane – by themselves; weir – war

15. THE LANG AWA SHIP
    canty ingle – cheerful fireplace

19. FOONDRY LANE
Juter – jute cargo ship; Battener – wood ship; ingins – onions; secks – sacks; shew – sew; claes – clothes; wulks – whelks

31. THE OVERGATE
bower – parlour or bedroom; waukrife – wakeful

32. THE BEEFCAN CLOSE
pooch – pocket; sark – shirt

33. BEWARE OF AN ABERDONIAN
glaikit – silly, thoughtless; jaud – old woman

37. THE DUNDEE LASSIE
iler – oiler; winder – a job on the *flett*

38. THE JUTE MILL SONG
cled – clothe

42. THE SPINNER'S WEDDING
gaffer – boss, foreman; flett – working platform; chanty – chamber pot; siller – silver (money)

43. JOHNNY SHAW'S A DECENT CHAP
chiel – lad; safter – weak person; aft – often

46. BLIN' HUGHIE
Kilmarnock – woven hat; toorie – bobble; ahint – behind; coothie – pleasant; ilka – each, every; thrapple – throat; happin – wavering; shoon – shoes; thrawn – twisted; tint – lost; chiels – lads; hame-ower – homesick; hinny-honey (hinny measure – love song); kittle – tickle, please

47. JENNY MARSHALL'S CANDY O
streicht – straight; rash – rush, reed; loon – fellow, lad; piece – sandwich; weety – wet; baubie – halfpenny

48. WORTHIES OF DUNDEE I
syne – then; dings – beats; snack mou' – sharp wit; limmer – loose woman; dilse and tangle – succulent seaweeds; leear – liar

51. INDYGO BLUE
middens – rubbish-heap; siver – drain

52. DONAL DON
tanterwallops – baggy, ragged clothing; smeeky – smokey, dark; pliskie – trick; braws – trousers; clorty – dirty; fyle – defile; sark – shirt; loupin – leaping (with dirt)

54. WORTHIES OF DUNDEE II
blate – shy; mixter maxter – mixed up; physog – face

58. SCOTS CALLAN O' BONNIE DUNDEE
hauver-meal bannock – oatmeal cake; dougl'd – dandle;
haffets – cheeks; simmer – summer; ee-brie – eyebrow;
big a bower – build a house; lav'd – lapped, washed;
wimplin' – rippling; cleed – clothe

59. JAMIE FRAE DUNDEE
may – lamb, sheep; laverock – lark; lint-white – linnet

67. THE IRON HORSE
ruggit – tugged; gar'd – made; kist – chest, box; stracht – straight;
chiels – chaps, lads; hale – whole; sic – such; fand – searched;
pooches – pockets; tint – lost; abeen – above

68. THE WIFE O' DUNDEE
soom – swim

70. I'LL AWA HAME
bide – stay; skelps – hits

73. THE BOMBIN RAID
Ally men – Germans

74. ROBBIE AND GRANNY
ilka – every; rushle – rattle; hirstled – wheezed; struisled – struggled;
neuk end – fireside

75. ANDRA CARNEGIE
pent – paint; ava – at all; maik – halfpenny, small gratuity

76. THE NICHT THAT OOR MAG HAD HER BAIRN
coo sharin – cow's dung; howdie – midwife; wame – stomach

77. CATHERINE STREET
greet – cry; skelp – a bit of land

80. WE'RE NO AWA TAE BIDE AWA
hauf – measure of whisky

Bibliography

Bronson, Bertrand *The Traditional Tunes of the Child Ballads,* 4 vols. (Princeton, N.J., 1959-72)

Brooksbank, Mary *Sidlaw Breezes* (Dundee, 1966; reprinted David Winter & Sons, 1982)

Brune, John and Cook, Gillian *The Roving Songster* (n.p., 1965)

Buchan, Norman *101 Scottish Songs* (Glasgow, 1962)

Buchan, Norman and Hall, Peter *The Scottish Folksinger* (Glasgow, 1973)

Cameron, David Keir *The Ballad and the Plough* (London, 1978)

Campbell, Alex *Songs* (Great Yarmouth, 1971)

Child, Francis J. *The English and Scottish Popular Ballads,* 5 vols. (Boston & New York, 1882-98; reprinted New York, 1965)

Creighton, Helen *Folksongs of Southern New Brunswick* (Toronto, 1950)

Christie, William *Traditional Ballad Airs* (Edinburgh, 1876)

Dallas, Karl *100 Songs of Toil* (n.p., n.d.)

Doerflinger, William M. *Songs of the Sailor and Lumberman* (New York, 1951)

Douglas, Sheila *Sing a Song of Scotland* (London, 1981)

The Dundee Market Crosses and Tolbooths (Dundee, 1901)

D'Urfey, Thomas *Pills to Purge Melancholy* (Reprint of 4th edition, London, 1876)

Folk Notes Magazine, No. 1, Aberdeen Folk Club (Aberdeen, 1969)

Ford, Robert *Song Histories* (Glasgow, 1900)

Ford, Robert *Vagabond Songs and Ballads of Scotland* (Paisley & London, 1899-1901)

Fowke, Edith Fulton *Traditional Singers and Songs from Ontario* (Hatboro, 1965)

Fraser, Amy Stewart *Dae ye min' Langsyne* (London, 1975)

Gatherer, William A. *Ballads High and Low* (London, 1975)

Gauldie, Enid *The Dundee Textile Industry, 1870-1885* (Scottish History Society, 1969)

Glen, John *Early Scottish Melodies* (Edinburgh, 1900)

Graham, C. Farquar *The Popular Songs and Melodies of Scotland* (Glasgow, 1893)

Greig, Gavin *Folk Song in Buchan and Folk Song of the North East* (Peterhead, 1907-11)

Hartwich, Veronica C. *Ale an' A'thin'* (Dundee, 1980)

Herd, David *The Ancient & Modern Scots Songs,* 2 vols. (1769) (Glasgow, 1869)

Hogg, James *The Jacobite Relics of Scotland,* 2 vols. (Edinburgh, 1819-21)

Hugill, Stan *Shanties from the Seven Seas* (London, 1961)

Hutchinson, R. E. *The Jacobite Rising of 1715* (Edinburgh, 1965)

Johnson, James *The Scots Musical Museums,* 2 vols. (Edinburgh, 1839)

Kay, Billy *Odyssey (Voices from Scotland's Recent Past)* (Edinburgh, 1980)

Kennedy, Peter *Folksongs of Britain and Ireland* (London, 1975)

Kerr's Cornkisters (Glasgow, 1950)

Kerr's Andy Stewart Album (Glasgow, 1961)

Kidson, Frank — *Traditional Tunes: A Collection of Ballad Airs* (Wakefield, 1970 – facsimile reprint of the Oxford 1891 edition)

Kidson, Frank — MS in Mitchell Library, Glasgow

Kinsley, James (ed.) — *The Oxford Book of Ballads* (Oxford, 1982)

MacColl, Ewan (ed.) — *The Shuttle and the Cage* (New York, 1965)

MacGregor, Jimmie — *Singing our Own* (Edinburgh, 1970)

Macintosh, Murdoch — *A History of Dundee* (Dundee, 1939)

McNeill, F. Marian — *The Silver Bough, Vol. 4 – Local Festivals of Scotland* (Glasgow, 1957)

Martin, George McG. — *Dundee Worthies* (Dundee, 1934)

Maxwell, Alexander — *The History of Old Dundee* (Edinburgh, 1884)

Millar, Alexander H. — *Haunted Dundee* (Dundee, 1923)

Millar, Alexander H. — *Glimpses of Old and New Dundee* (Dundee, 1925)

Municipal History of Dundee (Dundee, 1978)

Ord, John — *Bothy Songs and Ballads* (Paisley, 1930)

Ordnance Gazetter of Scotland, ed. Francis H. Groome (Edinburgh, 1884)

Outram, George — *Legal and Other Lyrics* (Edinburgh, 1888)

Palmer, Roy — *A Ballad History of England* (London, 1979)

Perkins, John — *Sagas of the Sea: Tales of Dundee's Maritime Past* (Dundee, 1976)

Phillips, David — *The Hungry Thirties* (Dundee, 1981)

Phillips, Douglas and Phillips, David *Dundee* (Dundee, 1980)

Raven, Jon — *Victoria's Inferno* (Wolverhampton, 1978)

Reinfeld, Fred — *Whales and Whaling* (n.p., n.d.)

Richards, Sam and Stubbs, Tish *The English Folksinger* (London, 1979)

Rogers, Rev. Charles — *The Scottish Minstrel* (Edinburgh, 1873)

Rymour Club, Edinburgh *Miscellanea,* Vol. 1 (Edinburgh, 1906-11)

Seeger, Peggy and MacColl, Ewan *The Singing Island* (London, 1960)

Sharp, Cecil J. — *English Folksongs from the Southern Appalachians* (London, 1932)

Shuldham-Shaw, Patrick and Lyle, Emily (eds.) *The Greig/Duncan Folksong Collection,* Vol. 1 (Aberdeen, 1981)

Skinner, Rev. W. C. — *The Barronie of Hilltowne, Dundee* (Dundee, 1927)

Smellie, Alexander — *Men of the Covenant* (London, 1911)

Smith, W. J. — *A History of Dundee* (Dundee, 1873; reprinted David Winter & Sons, 1973)

Thompson, J. Hannay *Dundee Harbour Trust – A Brief History* (Dundee, 1933)

Walker, William M. — *Juteopolis – Dundee and its Textile Workers, 1885-1923* (Edinburgh, 1979)

Warrack, Alexander (ed.) *Chambers Scots Dictionary* (Edinburgh, 1911)

Watlen, J. — *Collection of Scots Songs* (Glasgow, c. 1796)

Whitelaw, Alexander (ed). *The Book of Scottish Song* (Glasgow, 1866)

Index of Songs